My Garden

MY GARDEN

Selected from the letters and recollections of
Mary Russell Mitford

by Robyn Marsack

Illustrated by Pamela Kay

HOUGHTON MIFFLIN COMPANY
BOSTON

First published in Great Britain in 1990 by
Sidgwick & Jackson Limited
1 Tavistock Chambers, Bloomsbury Way, London WC1A 2SG

An Albion Book

Conceived, designed and produced by
The Albion Press Limited
P.O. Box 52, Princes Risborough, Aylesbury, Bucks HP17 9PR

Designer: Emma Bradford
Project co-ordinator: Elizabeth Wilkes
Photography: Tony Bryan ARPS

Pamela Kay thanks The Museum of Kent Rural Life, Maidstone,
Tyrwhitt-Drake Museum of Carriages, Maidstone and Lady Fitzwalter
of Goodnestone Park, Kent for allowing her garden to be used in
some of the paintings.

Typesetting and colour origination by York House, London
Printed and bound in Spain by Graficas Estella, S.A

CIP data is available.

For our mothers
Lydia Kay and Evelyn Marsack
PK & RM

Contents

INTRODUCTION

In 1849, Mary Russell Mitford wrote to an American friend that there were only two things of which she was 'immoderately proud', and one of them was her garden. She did not mention her literary activities in this connection: they were pursued from financial necessity, whereas the garden was a joy – though also hard work, and a source of anxiety, as gardeners will appreciate. How to protect – for example – two hundred prized geraniums?

> . . . withering, poor dears in the sun, and afraid of a thunder-shower; and we all began lamenting for the hundredth time that we could not devise a canvas awning to shelter them. 'Can't it be done in wood?' said Captain Gore, 'anything may be done in wood.' . . . on Tuesday, when I returned from my round of visits, I found the captain and six men erecting the machine, which is really the most serviceable and beautiful canopy ever devised.

Geraniums, and perhaps roses, were her favourites, but as this selection shows, most flowers win her approval, and wild flowers in particular. Her friend Henry Chorley, writing in the *Athenaeum* (26 October 1839), is sniffy about Pfauen-Insel and the attempt to create an 'English' garden: 'There is a greater variety of plants in one patch the size of a table, in Miss Mitford's flower garden, than in the whole open-air "policy" of the King of Prussia.'

By this time, Miss Mitford's name would have been familiar to the English reading public: *Our Village* was published in 1832, *Belford Regis* in 1835 and *Country Stories* in 1837. Each volume brought her dozens of letters of appreciation, and widened the circle of friends she maintained by letter. (Some days she wrote sixteen or more, in her often illegible hand, and complained in a letter of 1852 about not being able to count on a reply by return of post.) Mary Russell Mitford had not begun with these charming, humorous and observant sketches of country life, but with poems criticized in draft by Coleridge, and with historical dramas successfully performed in Drury Lane. Like the packed flowerbeds of her cottage gardens, her literary world is crowded and brilliant, and perhaps the only thing we can say in her father's favour was that he gave her the entrée into such a world.

George Mitford, from an ancient north country family, was orphaned at eight, and his youthful career is something of a mystery. He was certainly on the medical staff of a naval hospital a couple of years before he went to Alresford in Hampshire. There he was introduced to the local heiress, Mary Russell, whom he married in 1785. She was wealthy, plain and ten years his senior; he was impecunious, handsome, high-spirited and sociable. Their marriage appears to have been a happy one and Dr Mitford a devoted husband, but he was also a spendthrift and a gambler.

Their only surviving child, Mary, was born in Alresford in 1787. She had a comfortable childhood and was much petted by her parents. Mary could read by the time she was three; when the family moved to Reading in 1791, she was sent to the Abbey School. By 1795, Dr Mitford had worked his way through most of his wife's fortune (about £28,000) and decided to move to Lyme Regis, 'feeling with character-istic sanguineness that in a fresh place success would be certain'. Here they rented a fine house with a garden that Mary loved, with 'arbutus, passion-flowers, myrtles and moss-roses': 'it did not seem a place to be sad in'. Nevertheless it did not provide the luck Dr Mitford sought, and the financial situation was desperate. They removed to London, and somehow managed to live until an extraordinary stroke of luck. On her tenth birthday, Mary and her father were taking a walk and came across a shabby lottery office. Dr Mitford asked her to choose a ticket and, against his advice, she picked one whose number added up to ten. A week later, they learned that it was the winning ticket in the Irish lottery, worth £20,000. Dr Mitford had a dinner-service made, with his arms and the Irish harp and the number 2224 incorporated into the design. This fragile evidence, Mary later remarked, outlasted the money.

Still, she went back to school, this time in Chelsea, where she received a good education, especially in French and drama. Her parents returned to Reading, but Dr Mitford was determined to establish himself as a country gentleman. He bought an old farmhouse on the Basingstoke road, demolished it and had 'Bertram House' built by 1804, amidst sixty acres of land. Dr Mitford gambled in London and followed greyhounds round the county, making the acquaintance of William Cobbett and members of the Whig aristocracy. He was appointed magistrate in 1806, but by 1811 his affairs were in such chaos that the decision to sell Bertram House was taken.

Meanwhile Mary had been launched on her literary career, with the publication of *Miscellaneous Poems* (1810); despite a severe notice in the *Edinburgh Review*, a second augmented edition came out in 1811, followed by long narrative poems in 1811, 1812 and 1813. Dr Mitford certainly promoted these volumes in his useful London circle; his wife and daughter were left to deal with the creditors in Reading. Mary pleaded with her father to be told the exact financial situation, but he would not discuss it with her, and none of her sensible plans were ever put into operation.

Mary's pocket diary for the years 1819-23 is preserved in the British Library. There are only brief entries – 'At home – read Walpole's letters to Mrs Montagu – charming – wrote some more of my letter to Sir William Elford' – yet it may be observed that at this period she was reading two books a day, when time allowed. She occasionally went to London, and met eminent authors and artists of the day. The removal to Three Mile Cross – at first considered a temporary expedient – was a clear sign that her own efforts were essential for the family's support.

So she turned to writing plays, as well as sketches for ladies' magazines: 'I work as hard as a lawyer's clerk, and besides the natural loathing of pen and ink which that sort of drudgery cannot fail to inspire, I have really at present scarcely a moment to spare, even for the violets and primroses'. She did not foresee that it was the articles, rather than her tragedies *Julian*, *Foscari* and *Rienzi* that would bring her lasting fame and devoted readers, in America as well as Great Britain. The strain on her health was considerable, the more so when Mrs Mitford's health and mind gave way, and it fell to Mary to nurse her as well as run the household. The garden was her indulgence and refuge, as she wrote to Haydon in 1824:

> All and every part is untrimmed, antique, weather-stained and homely as can be imagined – gratifying the eye by its exceeding picturesqueness, and the mind by the certainty that no pictorial effect was intended – that it owes all its charms to 'rare accident'. My father laughs at my passionate love of my little garden – and perhaps you will laugh too; but I assure you it's a 'bonny bit' of earth as was ever crammed full of lilies and roses . . .

Mrs Mitford died in 1830, but her daughter had little space for grieving, having to earn money for the expenses of her illness and funeral.

In these decades of unremitting work, intermittent ill-health and constant financial anxieties, the rare trips to London must have been a welcome break in her intellectual isolation. In 1836, she reported to her father a dinner party with 'Mr Wordsworth, whom I *love* – he is an adorable old man'; while the Duke of Devonshire 'brought me a splendid nosegay of lilies of the valley (a thousand flowers without leaves – I hope I shall find mine in their prime) and moss roses . . .', and Edwin Landseer offered to paint her dog. It was a particular boon to make a new friend on that visit, Elizabeth Barrett. At this time it was the older woman who had the literary reputation that the poet was later to gain. Miss Barrett never understood quite the extent to which Miss Mitford suffered under practical cares, and after her marriage – which came as a complete surprise to her friend – they were naturally never as close.

> I have a great basket full of [EBB's] letters, for before Mr Browning stole her from me we used to write to each other at least twice a week, and by dint of intimacy and frequency of communication could, I think, have found enough matter for a correspondence of twice a day. It was really talk, fireside talk, neither better nor worse, assuming necessarily a form of permanence – gossip daguerreotyped.

This mutually sustaining sympathy was augmented by Miss Mitford's almost overwhelming supply of flowers, and the gift of the famous spaniel, Flush.

When Dr Mitford died in 1842, after four years of illness, he left debts of nearly £800 and a daughter broken in health. It is astonishing that her correspondence over all this time is on the whole cheerful, never self-pitying, and unfailingly loving in its references to her father. *The Times* and the *Morning Chronicle* published an appeal for a Public Subscription: 'That which would fall with a crushing weight upon one solitary and almost destitute woman, will be but little felt when divided among the affluent and the many.' The amount thus raised came to £1,600, the donors including the young Queen Victoria (anonymously), members of the aristocracy, fellow writers such as Maria Edgeworth and Fanny Trollope, and old friends. It was enough to clear the debts and establish a small pension.

At last she had a sufficient income, could entertain friends at the newly decorated cottage, garden to her heart's content, go to London to visit Miss Barrett. At the end of 1844 she organized the 290 village children to see the Queen, on a visit to the Duke of Wellington at nearby Strathfieldsaye, after which they all returned to her house, where the gentlefolks had sandwiches and cakes and wine; and where the children had each a bun as large as a soup-plate, made doubly nice as well as doubly large, a glass of wine, and a mug of ale. All this seems little enough, but the ecstasy of the children made it much.

In the winter of 1845, she is writing cheerfully to Emily Jephson –

in the midst of a fall of snow, a foot deep at least, which is bad for me who hate dirt like a cat, and yet shall have to wade through it for the rest of the month; my daily walks being not only the necessity of existence to me, so far as health is concerned, but also the chief means of my social pleasures; for since I have made the grand discovery that a lantern is as good as a moon, I trot about at night with a maid, not merely to country neighbours but to lectures and concerts in Reading, where I have a whole Mechanics' Institute as an object of interest and pleasure.

The cottage was damp, however, and aggravated her rheumatism, so after much uncertainty she moved to Swallowfield in 1851. Not long afterwards, she was in a carriage accident and her 'personal activity' – her other cause for immoderate pride – was reduced to nothing by the injury to her spine. James Payn, the novelist and editor of the *Cornhill* magazine, met her at this time.

I expected to find the authoress of *Our Village* in a most pictures-que cottage, overgrown with honeysuckle and roses, and set in an old fashioned garden. . . . It was a cottage, but not a pretty one, placed where three roads met, with only a piece of green before it. But if the dwelling disappointed me, the owner did not. I was ushered upstairs . . . into a small apartment, lined with books from floor to ceiling and fragrant with flowers; its tenant rose from her armchair with difficulty, but with a sunny smile and a charming manner bade me welcome. My father had been an old friend of hers, and she spoke of my home and my belongings as only a woman can speak of these things. Then we plunged *in medias res* – into men and books.

Under these circumstances, Miss Mitford managed to write a novel, *Atherton* (1854) – not her best work, but immensely popular, and praised by John Ruskin as having 'in common with all your works – an indescribable perfume and sweetness, as of lily of the valley and honey, utterly unattained by any other writer'.

Mary Russell Mitford died on 10 January 1855, with Lady Russell, one of her oldest friends, at her side. Elizabeth Barrett Browning's assessment of her, often quoted, bears quoting again:

> . . . she is herself better and stronger than any of her books; and her letters and conversation show more grasp of intellect and general power than would be inferable from her finished composi-tions. . . . In her works, however, through all the beauty there is a clear vein of sense, and a quickness of observation which takes the character of a refined shrewdness. . . . And is she not besides most intensely a woman, and an Englishwoman?

ROBYN MARSACK

Notes on Miss Mitford's Correspondents

Elizabeth Barrett Browning *(1806-61)* The two women wrote a prodigious number of letters to each other, the poet's being collected in *The Letters of Elizabeth Barrett Browning to Mary Russell Mitford 1836-1854*, edited by Meredith B. Raymond and Mary Rose Sullivan (3 vols, 1983). They first met in 1836, when MRM was forty-nine, and it would seem true that after her parents, Elizabeth Barrett was the person she most loved.

Charles Boner *(1815-70)* Tutor to the two elder sons of John Constable, then to the children of Prince von Thurn und Taxis at Ratisbon. He translated from the German version many of Hans Christian Andersen's fairy tales, dedicating *The Nightingale and Other Tales* (1846) to MRM. 'Mr Boner is a most accomplished man. He came to me eight or nine years ago from Mr Wordsworth, and we have been fast friends ever since.'

Sir William Elford *(?1746-1836)* A friend of Dr Mitford's, created baronet by Pitt in 1800, MP and Recorder for Plymouth, where he was partner in a bank. He was fond of poetry and painting, and a member of the Royal Society. MRM obviously worked carefully at her early letters to this distinguished man, but relaxed as their friendship ripened.

Revd William Harness *(1790-1846)* The son of Mrs Mitford's trustee, and later trustee to MRM, and instrumental in obtaining a pension for her. He published an edition of Shakespeare in 1825 and himself wrote plays.

Benjamin Robert Haydon *(1776-1846)* An historical painter, friend of Keats, Wordsworth et al., and of MRM since 1817. After he killed himself in June 1846, the family asked MRM to write his life, but she did not wish to take on such a demanding task. His portrait of her is in the Reading Museum. 'He was a sort of Benvenuto Cellini; or rather he was like Shakespeare's description of the Dauphin's horse – "all air and fire . . . ",' MRM wrote to a friend in 1852.

Mrs Hoare This lady wrote to MRM on the publication of *Recollections of a Literary Life* and their correspondence continued until MRM's death. Mrs Hoare was the author of a collection of short stories, *Shamrock Leaves* (1851?).

Mrs Barbara Hofland *(1770-1844)* A prolific author of over seventy works, mainly novels, she also added descriptions to her husband's engraved sketches. He was the landscape painter Thomas Christopher Hofland, of whom MRM wrote, 'he talks pictures and paints poems'. She described Mrs Hofland as 'womanly to her fingers' ends, and as truth-telling and independent as a skylark'.

Emily Jephson *(b. 1802)* The grandneice of Robert Jephson, the Irish dramatist (1736-1803), she was brought up by the family of Maria Edgeworth, the novelist. She lived mainly in Ireland and seems to have been a keen gardener. MRM wrote that she was 'one of the most cultivated women that I have ever known, with a sweetness and simplicity of character, a charm of mind and manner which really make one forget how very clever she is'.

Mrs Jennings I have not been able to discover anything about her.

Mrs Acton Tindal *(d. 1879)* Born Henrietta Harrison, she published a novel *The Heirs of Blackridge Manor* under the pseudonym of Diana Butler, and as Henrietta E. Tindal two volumes of poetry, *Lines and Leaves* (1848) and *Rhymes and Legends* (1879). In 1847, MRM wrote of her to Charles Boner, 'she is a most sweet and lovely blonde . . . I think she will attain a great popularity. Her poems have a force and finish of no common order.'

John Ruskin *(1819-1900)* MRM met Ruskin in 1847, and wrote to a friend that he was 'certainly the most charming person that I have ever known . . . just what if one had a son one should have dreamt of his turning out, in mind, manner, conversation, everything.' Ruskin and his father sent her wine in her last years of illness, and he wrote often and sent her books. See Elizabeth Lee's edition of *Mary Russell Mitford: Correspondence with Charles Boner and John Ruskin* (1914).

Thomas Noon Talfourd *(1795-1854)* Trained in law and later a circuit judge and MP for Reading, Talfourd's real interest was literature. He was Charles Lamb's friend and biographer, and Dickens dedicated *Pickwick Papers* to him. The recipe printed here is not typical of the extensive correspondence between him and MRM, which centred on her plays and his efforts to negotiate their performance.

The printed collections of letters, besides those mentioned above, are: *The Life of Mary Russell Mitford* edited by A.G. L'Estrange (3 vols, 1870); *Letters of Mary Russell Mitford*, Second Series, edited by Henry Chorley (2 vols, 1872); *The Friendships of Mary Russell Mitford*, edited by A.G. L'Estrange (2 vols, 1882). There is a biography, *Mary Russell Mitford*, by Vera Watson (1949). Where possible, the letters in this selection were checked against originals in Reading Public Library and the British Library; manuscripts in the John Rylands Library (Manchester) and the Bodleian Library (Oxford) were also consulted. I am especially grateful to helpful librarians in the Local Studies section of the Reading Public Library.

It was a great, warm, outflowing heart, and the head was worthy of the heart. . . . There might have been, as you suggest, a somewhat different development elsewhere than in Berkshire – not very different though – souls don't grow out of the ground.

I agree with you that she was stronger and wider in her conversation than in her books. Oh! I have said so a hundred times. The heat of human sympathy seemed to bring out her powerful vitality, rustling all over with laces and flowers.

Elizabeth Barrett Browning to
John Ruskin, 5 November 1855

To Sir William Elford, Bickham, Plymouth

Bertram House, 17 April 1812

I am no naturalist – not for lack of inclination, but from a real want of physical powers; for though I have, to be sure, two ears and two eyes like other people, so miserably defective are these organs, that neither of them would serve me to distinguish a tomtit from a robin redbreast; and yet in spite of this misfortune I read Mr White's book [A *Natural History of Selborne*] with unceasing delight. I really think that I have read it half a dozen times in my life. This appears extraordinary, but I believe that, in Mr White's case, truth is the talisman. There is an air of reality in his descriptions which I meet with nowhere else; and we poets may talk as we will of Fiction, but the gipsy is never attractive excepting when she borrows the garments of truth. . . .

I am glad you will have something at Bickham which has once been here. I shall always be happy to be remembered by my kind and excellent correspondent; and I think I had rather be recalled to his memory by flowers than by anything else. This refers exclusively to the evening primrose plants, of which, luckily for my purpose, Mr Swallow had none, and which are therefore sent from hence. You must not expect any delicate poetical flower – they are only fit for the borders of shrubberies and such places, where I think you will like them. The blossoms expand about half an hour or perhaps rather more, after sunset. In truth, nothing can be more vulgar than my taste in flowers, for which I have a passion. I like scarcely any but the common ones. First and best I love violets, and primroses, and cowslips, and wood anemones, and the whole train of field flowers; then roses of every kind and colour, especially the great cabbage rose; then the blossoms of the lilac and laburnum, the horse-chestnut, the asters, the jasmine, and the honeysuckle; and to close the list, lilies of the valley, sweet peas, and the red pinks which are found in cottagers' gardens. This is my confession of faith. Pray don't betray me. Your more elegant collection was sent off by Tromont's coach last night. . . . Adieu, my dear sir!

To Sir William Elford, 18 Bury Street, St. James's

Bertram House, 22 April 1812

. . . I am highly flattered to find that you think my letters worth preserving. I keep yours as choice as the monks were wont to keep the relics of their saints; and about sixty years hence your grandson or great-grandson will discover in the family archives some notice of such a collection, and will send to the grandson of my dear cousin Mary (for as I intend to die an old maid, I shall make her heiress to all my property, i.e. my MSS.) for these inestimable remains of his venerable ancestor. And then, you know, my letters will be rummaged out, and the whole correspondence will be sorted and transcribed, and sent to the press, adorned with portraits, and *fac similes*, and illustrated by lives of the authors, beginning with the register of their birth, and ending with their epitaphs. Then it will come forth into the world, and set all the men a-crowing and talking over their old nonsense (with more show of reason, however, than ordinary) about the superiority of the sex. What a fine job the transcriber of my letters will have. I hope the booksellers of those days will be liberal and allow the poor man a good price for his trouble; no one but an unraveller of state cyphers can possibly accomplish it.

What you say respecting my choice of flowers only proves that your taste is as humble as mine. But I do assure you that a jury of florists would give a verdict against us for bad taste in any country in Christendom. Why, here is my dear Mama, watching with careful eyes the unfolding of a magnificent camellia japonica, and here is our good neighbour, Mrs Reeve (ah! ah! fair lady! I will teach you to steal into a room and look over my shoulder!) – here is Mrs Reeve who ought to love what she so much resembles, and yet cannot endure the sight of a rose, except those which her gardener brings in February and March from her hot-house to her drawing-room; poor sickly flowers, which have never been fanned by the air of heaven, nor refreshed by any showers but those from a watering-pot. Ask either of these ladies (especially the last, for Mama loves all that is good and all that is beautiful, whether in a field or a garden, a cottage window or a drawing-room) what flowers they admire, and they will answer you by a thousand unspeakable names of bulbs from Caffraria, and shrubs from the American mountains. For my part, I am delighted at this coincidence of taste between us. I place flowers in the very first rank of simple pleasures; and I have no very good opinion of the hard worldly people who take no delight in them.

Whitley Cottage, Friday

Did you ever happen to write with a pen twenty years old, and just a drop and a half of ink, in the midst of a universal cleckit of female tongues? If you never did, you are no competent judge of my present situation, and to describe it is impossible. Who can describe the almost inconceivable *mélange* of a true female gossip; where dress and music, dancing and preaching, pelisses and beaux, flowers and scandal, all meet together, like the oil and vinegar of a salad? It must, however, plead my apology for all blunders.

To Sir William Elford, Bickham, Plymouth

Bertram House, 4 January 1814

Did you ever see such beautiful weather as we have had for the last week? I doubt, though, whether with you – so near the sea and in a milder climate – the weather may have deserved the epithet I have bestowed on it. Here the scene has been lovely beyond any winter piece I ever beheld – a world formed of something much whiter than ivory – as white, indeed, as snow – but carved with a delicacy, a lightness, a precision to which the massy ungraceful tottering snow could never pretend. Rime was the architect. Every tree every shrub every blade of grass was clothed with its pure incrustations, but so thinly so delicately clothed, that every twig every fibre every ramification remained perfect, alike indeed in colour, but displaying in form, to the fullest extent, the endless infinite variety of Nature. This diversity of form never appeared so striking as now that all the difference of colour was at an end – never so lovely as when breaking with its soft yet well-defined outline on a sky rather grey than blue – It was a scene which really defies description. The shrubberies were slightly different – there some little modification of colour obtruded itself – The saffron-tinted leaves of the cut-leaved oak fringed round with their snowy border – The rich seed-vessels of the sweet-briar blushing through their light veil, and the flexible branches of the broom, weighed down, yet half unloaded of their fine burden and peeping out in their bright verdure like spring in the lap of winter; all this was yesterday enchanting – Today it is levelled and annihilated by the heavy uniformity of snow, of which just enough has fallen to spoil the walks, the roads, and the prospects. By the bye, I ought not to quarrel with this fall since it proves me weather-wise – A shoemaker came here yesterday to whom after paying his bill I said, by way of saying something, 'I think it looks like snow.' 'Yes, Ma'am,' said the man, *'rime always does.'* . . .

To Sir William Elford, Bickham, Plymouth

Bertram House, 19 January 1818

. . . Did I ever talk to you about Bear Wood? A spot about six miles from us of remarkable beauty – It was, as you might imagine from the name a beech wood – very old, and blended into the Commons which every way surrounded it by old stunted ragged beech trees, half stripped of their branches, growing first in straggling clumps and then scattered singly, forming the most picturesque and natural union with the bare and barren heath – When you got into the thicker part of the wood it was enchanting – large tangled masses of huge trees and thick underwood, holly bramble and fern, with all their accompaniments of wood flowers – broken by winding green paths – some formed naturally by the sheep, some purposely made by the hunters – for it abounded in game – nowhere level, but in one part descending abruptly to a deep long narrow glen – filled with one of those forest pools of which the effect is so beautiful – where the clear water seems placed like a mirror to catch the light, and reflect the deep-blue sky – Nothing could be so delightful as to stand on a sunny autumn day on the most level side of the water and look across the pool up to that amphitheatre of trees in their regular confusion, with their shining bark and their leaves changing from green to orange – It was within *donkey-cart distance* of Mr Webb's, and Mary and I used to take books and work, and sit there for whole mornings – About a year ago, it was sold, under the Forest Inclosure Act, to Mr Walter, one of the editors of the Times newspaper – He immediately resolved to build there and employed a certain Mr Crabtree as his agent, steward &c. – The first operation performed by Mr Crabtree was to cut down all and every one of the straggling old beech trees, whether single or in clumps, rounding the wood territory as completely and as smoothly as ever Buonaparte rounded the territory of some favoured king – the next, to make in two directions and across two commons a fine level straight gravel road to the wood, nicely bordered by a pretty little plantation of larches and firs. – In about a month down came Mr Walter and a landscape gardener (name forgotten) who

execrated poor Mr Crabtree's cutting-downs, and as it was impossible to make the trees grow again outside the wood, contented himself with forming magnificent plans for the interior. Accordingly he formed a plan for a lake where the pool used to be, or rather, for two lakes united in the middle by a cascade!! (Really it is well for the man that his name is forgotten!) and sixty persons were set to work to dig and trench and level for this magnificent design! All the spring, all the summer, all the autumn were these people at work – and now Mr Walter (either by the benefit of his own lights, or by the advice of some third professor . . .) having discovered that these lakes would spoil his place, has set all his 60 workmen to fill them up again – intending to have instead a small natural rivulet winding along the glen. I dare say he will come back to the pool. How often one is reminded of that admirable and philosophical distich 'The King of France with twenty thousand men – Marched up the hill and then marched down again!'

I am very glad to hear so excellent an account of my noble namesakes. I always thought this Duke of Bedford a much finer character than his celebrated predecessor. His brother-in-law, Mr Palmer, has just made me a very magnificent present. There is but one place in all Berkshire which has a really fine commanding prospect, and this is a turfy, almost inaccessible hill, called Finchamstead Ridges. Thither, at the risk of our necks, did Mr Webb and I clamber last autumn by the help of a gig and a blood horse, and I was in one of my ecstasies about it when we came home to dinner. Well, this was in the Inclosure Act too, and Mr Palmer bought it, and he has offered me six acres for a cottage and a garden and a field for a cow.

Only think of my being a lady of landed property! Was ever poetess so rich! Now, if I could but scrape together money enough for my cottage, what an independent person I should be! How much would it take to build a real cottage? Would a hundred pounds do? But it might just as well be a thousand; I should get the one as soon as the other. You must not think this splendid donation of our dear May-pole of a candidate a bribe. I am neither elector nor electress.

Was there ever such strange weather! Yesterday, going to Wokingham, I picked four primroses full blown in a ditch by the roadside, and Papa sometime last month found a robin's nest with three eggs in it.

To Sir William Elford, Bickham, Plymouth

Bertram House, 14 June 1818

Pleasant sensations always remind me of you, my ever kind friend – there are particular atmospheres which one associates, one scarcely knows why, with different people, the cold and the foggy and the rainy – and the dry-hot – yours is, I think, the *fresh* – the light cool breeze which comes so pleasantly after a warm oppressive day. Do you like to be turned into air? Well, I am just come from a walk – if walk it may be called, which was merely a zig-zag kind of progress from the rose bushes to the honeysuckles, from the honeysuckles to the syringa tree – from the syringa to the acacia and from the acacia back to the roses. – I have been gathering sweets by night as the bee gathers them by day – the luxury of that fresh growing perfume a flowering shrub in full bloom is to me the greatest of all enjoyments – and of all flowers the white acacia is, I think, the most fragrant; and of all white acacias, one which is my pet tree is the most laden with blossoms; and of all evenings in which to stand under it, this has been the pleasantest – a light wind shaking down the loosely hung florets upon my pet Mossy's black neck – and Mossy looking up and half-suspecting some evil design till another shower seemed to explain the cause and remove his fears. My dear Sir William, I cannot think how any one who was 'of woman born', who did not spring ready armed out of the earth, like Minerva, can possibly submit himself and all his ancestors – fathers, mothers, brothers, sisters, wife, cousins of all degrees of kindred – to the horrible ordeal of a contested election! And only think how it fares with our dear candidate, whose wife (Lady Madelina, the eldest daughter of the Duke of Gordon), has the misfortune to have a pension, and whose uncle, Tyshe Palmer, senior, had the *honour* to be transported for sedition! Think of that! However, in spite of the pension and the transportation, he will gain the victory; we are quite sure of it – quite. Besides, we have all the – the – (dear me, I was going to say mob) – all the gentlemen porters, and gentlemen chimney-sweepers, and so forth, with us; and the Weylandites, the moment they come into the street, are over-crowed; and we are cheered and huzzaed, and drawn about and squeezed to death, and everything that is charming and pretty.

To Sir William Elford, Bickham, Plymouth
Bertram House (this pen won't write), 26 September 1819

. . . First of all, to answer your kind questions. I can't tell where we go, nor
when. There is no more chancery suit, that is certain; but the writings are
not drawn, money not paid, and so forth; and till then we shall remain here.
The *where* is even more uncertain than the *when*. I have not, however, any
notion that we shall migrate far from this neighbourhood; and, to tell you the
truth, am desperately afraid of the famous and patriotic borough of Reading,
which papa likes, for its newspaper and its justice-rooms and its elections;
and which I dislike for various negative reasons.

A town of negations that Reading is – no trees – no flowers – no green
fields – no wit – no literature – no elegance! Neither the society of London
nor the freedom of the country. We never say a word about it, for or against –
never mention the illustrious dull town; but I expect that some fine morning
Papa will come back and have taken a house there. And my only comfort is,
that (as I foreknow), after a little grumbling and pining at the transplant-
ation (dear me! I was just going to write 'transportation' – I beg Botany Bay's
pardon) – after a little shrivelling and writhing just at first – I shall settle in
the new earth, put out fresh leaves, and be as sound at heart as a transplanted
cabbage, or any other housewifely vegetable. The middle course, and that to
which I believe my dear Mama inclines, is a cottage within a walk of
Reading. This, if such a thing could be procured, I should like exceedingly.
It would suit us all. Wherever we go, you shall hear all about it – never, I
hope, out of your way, my dear Sir William. It would be too much to lose at
once our friends and our nightingales; and at or near Reading we shall be
more in your road than ever.

from 'The First Primrose', *Our Village*

Ah, May is bounding forward! Her silly heart leaps at the sight of the old place [Bertram House] – and so, in good truth does mine. What a pretty place it was, – or rather, how pretty I thought it! I suppose I should have thought any place so where I had spent eighteen happy years. But it was really pretty. A large, heavy, white house, in the simplest style, surrounded by fine oaks and elms, and tall massy plantations shaded down into a beautiful lawn by wild overgrown shrubs, bowery acacias, ragged sweet-briers, promontories of dog-wood, and Portugal laurel, and bays, overhung by laburnum and bird-cherry; a long piece of water letting light into the picture, and looking just like a natural stream, the banks as rude and wild as the shrubbery, interspersed with broom, and furze, and bramble and pollard oaks covered with ivy and honeysuckle; the whole enclosed by an old mossy park paling, and terminating in a series of rich meadows, richly planted. This is an exact description of the home which, three years ago, it nearly broke my heart to leave. What a tearing up by the root it was! I have pitied cabbage-plants and celery, and all transplantable things, ever since; though, in common with them, and with other vegetables, the first agony of the transportation being over, I have taken such firm and tenacious hold of my new soil, that I would not for the world be pulled up again, even to be restored to the old beloved ground; – not even if its beauty were undiminished, which is by no means the case; for in those three years it has thrice changed masters, and every successive possessor has brought the curse of improvement upon the place: so that between filling up the water to cure dampness, cutting down trees to let in prospects, planting to keep them out, shutting up windows to darken the inside of the house, (by which means one end looks precisely as an eight of spades would do that should have the misfortune to lose one of his corner pips,) and building colonnades to lighten the out, added to a general clearance of pollards, and brambles, and ivy, and honeysuckles, and park palings, and irregular shrubs, the poor place is so transmogrified, that if it had its old looking-glass, the water, back again, it would not know its own face.

And yet I love to haunt round about it: so does May. Her particular attraction is a certain broken bank full of rabbit burrows, into which she insinuates her long pliant head and neck, and tears her pretty feet by vain scratchings: mine is a warm sunny hedge-row, in the same remote field, famous for early flowers. Never was a spot more variously flowery: primroses yellow, lilac white, violets of either hue, cowslips, oxlips, arums, orchises, wild hyacinths, ground ivy, pansies, strawberries, heart's-ease, formed a small part of the Flora of that wild hedge-row. How profusely they covered the sunny open slope under the weeping birch, 'the lady of the woods' – and how often have I started to see the early innocent brown snake, who loved the spot as well as I did, winding along the young blossoms, or rustling amongst the fallen leaves! There are primrose leaves already, and short green buds, but no flowers; not even in that furze cradle so full of roots, where they used to blow as in a basket. No, my May, no rabbits! no primroses! We may as well get over the gate into the woody winding lane, which will bring us home again.

Here we are, making the best of our way between the old elms that arch so solemnly overhead, dark and sheltered even now. They say that a spirit haunts this deep pool – a white lady without a head. I cannot say that I have seen her, often as I have paced this lane at deep midnight, to hear the nightingales, and look at the glow-worms; – but there, better and rarer than a thousand ghosts, dearer even than nightingales or glow-worms, there is a primrose, the first of the year; a tuft of primroses, springing in yonder sheltered nook, from the mossy roots of an old willow, and living again in the clear bright pool. Oh, how beautiful they are – three fully blown, and two bursting buds! How glad I am I came this way! They are not to be reached. Even Jack Rapley's love of the difficult and the unattainable would fail him here: May herself could not stand on that steep bank. So much the better. Who would wish to disturb them? There they live in their innocent and fragrant beauty, sheltered from the storms, and rejoicing in the sunshine, and looking as if they could feel their happiness. Who would disturb them? Oh, how glad I am I came this way home!

To Mrs Hofland, Ullswater

Three Mile Cross, 11 April 1820

Your kind and welcome letter, my dearest Mrs Hofland, found me quite recovering from the bustle and discomposure of removal. We are three good miles from Reading. Indeed, I have so lively a sense of my escape in not being planted in the midst of that intolerable town, that much of the natural sorrow I should have felt at leaving a home so beloved was absorbed by the comforting reflection that I should still remain amongst shady lanes and quiet meadows. After all, we are not quite transplanted yet, – only 'laid by the heels', as the gardeners say. This place is a mere *pied à terre* till we can suit ourselves better; and my Reading-phobia is kept up by the dread that 'suit ourselves better', means (being translated) get a house there. In the mean-time, this place is a fine lesson of condensation, which, to say the truth, we all needed, Mama being as diffuse and elaborate in her tidiness as I in my litter; Papa unable to tell a short story; and Papa's daughter, as you, my dear friend, know to your cost, equally unable to write a short letter. Yes, we shall be greatly benefited by the compression – though at present the squeeze sits upon us as uneasily as tight stays, and is almost as awkward-looking. One of my great objections to small rooms is their extreme unbecomingness to a person of my enormity. There I sit in our little parlour, like a blackbird in a goldfinch's cage – filling it; the room seems all me; nevertheless we are really getting very comfortable, and falling into our old habits with all imaginable ease. Papa has already amused himself by committing a disorderly person, the pest of the Cross, and suspending the constable for appearing before him with a bloody cockscomb. Mama has converted an old dairy into a most commodious storeroom. I have stuffed the rooms with books, and the garden with flowers, and lost my only key. Lucy has made a score of new acquain-tances, and picked up a few lovers; and the great white cat, after appearing exceedingly disconsolate and out of his wits for a day or two, has given full proof of resuming his old warlike and predatory habits, by being lost all the morning in a large rat-hole, and stealing the milk for our tea this afternoon.

from 'Whitsun-Eve', *Our Village*

The pride of my heart and the delight of my eyes is my garden. Our house, which is in dimensions very much like a bird-cage, and might, with almost equal convenience, be laid on a shelf, or hung up in a tree, would be utterly unbearable in warm weather, were it not that we have a retreat out of doors, – and a very pleasant retreat it is. To make my readers comprehend it, I must describe our whole territories.

Fancy a small plot of ground, with a pretty low irregular cottage at one end; a large granary, divided from the dwelling by a little court running along one side; and a long thatched shed, open towards the garden, and supported by wooden pillars, on the other. The bottom is bounded, half by an old wall, and half by an old paling, over which we see a pretty distance of woody hills. The house, granary, wall, and paling, are covered with vines, cherry-trees, roses, honeysuckles, and jessamines, with great clusters of tall hollyhocks running up between them; a large elder overhanging the little gate, and a magnificent bay-tree, such a tree as shall scarcely be matched in these parts, breaking with its beautiful conical form the horizontal lines of the buildings. This is my garden; and the long pillared shed, the sort of rustic arcade, which runs along one side, parted from the flower-beds by a row of rich geraniums, is our out-of-door drawing-room.

I know nothing so pleasant as to sit there on a summer afternoon, with the western sun flickering through the great elder-tree, and lighting up our gay parterres, where flowers and flowering shrubs are set as thick as grass in a field, a wilderness of blossom, interwoven, intertwined, wreathy, garlandy, profuse beyond all profusion, where we may guess that there is such a thing as mould, but never see it. I know nothing so pleasant as to sit in the shade of that dark bower, with the eye resting on that bright piece of colour, lighted so gloriously by the evening sun, now catching a glimpse of the little birds as they fly rapidly in and out of their nests – for there are always two or three birds-nests in the thick tapestry of cherry-trees, honeysuckles, and China-roses, which covers our walls – now tracing the gay gambols of the common butterflies as they sport around the dahlias; now watching that rarer moth,

which the country people, fertile in pretty names, call the bee-bird; that bird-like insect, which flutters in the hottest days over the sweetest flowers, inserting its long proboscis into the small tube of the jessamine, and hovering over the scarlet blossoms of the geranium, whose bright colour seems reflected on its own feathery breast: that insect which seems so thoroughly a creature of the air, never at rest; always, even when feeding, self-poised, and self-supported, and whose wings, in their ceaseless motion, have a sound so deep, so full, so lulling, so musical. Nothing so pleasant as to sit amid that mixture of the flower and the leaf, watching the bee-bird! Nothing so pretty to look at as my garden! It is quite a picture; only unluckily it resembles a picture in more qualities than one, – it is fit for nothing but to look at. One might as well think of walking in a bit of framed canvass. There are walks to be sure – tiny paths of smooth gravel, by courtesy called such – but they are so overhung by roses and lilies, and such gay encroachers – so over-run by convolvulus, and heart's-ease, and mignonette, and other sweet stragglers, that, except to edge through them occasionally, for the purposes of planting, or weeding, or watering, there might as well be no paths at all. Nobody thinks of walking in my garden. Even May glides along with a delicate and trackless step, like a swan through the water; and we, its two-footed denizens, are fain to treat it as if it were really a saloon, and go out for a walk towards sun-set, just as if we had not been sitting in the open air all day.

What a contrast from the quiet garden to the lively street! Saturday night is always a time of stir and bustle in our village, and this is Whitsun-Eve, the pleasantest Saturday of all the year, when London journeymen and servant lads and lasses snatch a short holiday, to visit their families. A short and precious holiday, the happiest and liveliest of any; for even the gambols and merry-makings of Christmas offer but a poor enjoyment, compared with the rural diversions, the Mayings, revels, and cricket-matches of Whitsuntide.

We ourselves are to have a cricket-match on Monday, not played by the men, who, since a certain misadventure with the Beech-hillers, are, I am sorry to say, rather chap-fallen, but by the boys, who, zealous for the honour of their parish, and headed by their bold leader, Ben Kirby, marched in a body to our antagonists' ground the Sunday after our melancholy defeat, challenged the boys of that proud hamlet, and beat them out and out on the spot. Never was a more signal victory. Our boys enjoyed this triumph with so little moderation that it had like to have produced a very tragical catastrophe. The captain of the Beech-hill youngsters, a capital bowler, by name Amos Stone, enraged past all bearing by the crowing of his adversaries, flung the ball at Ben Kirby with so true an aim, that if that sagacious leader had not warily ducked his head when he saw it coming, there would probably have been a coroner's inquest on the case, and Amos Stone would have been tried for manslaughter. He let fly with such vengeance, that the cricket-ball was found embedded in a bank of clay five hundred yards off, as if it had been a cannon shot. Tom Coper and Farmer Thackum, the umpires, both say that they never saw so tremendous a ball. If Amos Stone live to be a man (I mean to say, if he be not hanged first) he'll be a pretty player. He is coming here on Monday with his party to play the return match, the umpires having respectively engaged, Farmer Thackum that Amos shall keep the peace, Tom Coper that Ben shall give no unnecessary or wanton provocation – a nicely worded and lawyer-like clause, and one that proves that Tom Coper hath his doubts of the young gentleman's discretion; and, of a truth, so have I. I would not be Ben Kirby's surety, cautiously as the security is worded, – no! not for a white double dahlia, the present object of my ambition.

To B.R. Haydon, 8 Paddington Green

Three Mile Cross, 1 May 1820

. . . I will not talk politics on May-day – this day of fairs and flowers. I am going to Reading Fair myself by-and-by, in a real market-cart, which will be delightful – and I have already been cowsliping. Are you fond of field flowers? They are my passion – even more, I think, than greyhounds or books. This country is eminently flowery. Besides all the variously-tinted primroses and violets in singular profusion, we have all sorts of orchises and arums; the delicate wood anemone; the still more delicate wood sorrel, with its lovely purple veins meandering over the white drooping flower; the field tulip, with its rich chequer-work of lilac and crimson, and the sun shining through the leaves as through old painted glass; the ghostly field star of Bethlehem (did you ever see that rare and ghost-like flower? Dr Clarke mentions having found it on a tumulus, which he took for the tomb of Ajax, in the Troad); wild lilies of the valley; and the other day I found a field completely surrounded by wild periwinkles. They ran along the hedge for nearly a quarter of a mile; to say nothing of the sculptural beauty of the white water lily and the golden clusters of the golden ranunculus. Yes, this is really a country of flowers, and so beautiful just now, that there is no making up one's mind to leave it; though, by dint of staying in it, one's 'wits get as mossy as the pales in an old orchard' – as somebody said of somebody – Old Aubrey Hobbes of Malmesbury, I believe.

Adieu, my dear sir. I am just going to set off on my expedition to the fair, to buy ribands and see the wild beasts. Adieu.

To Sir William Elford, Bickham, Plymouth
Three Mile Cross, September – I don't know what – but the last.
How many days has September?

. . . How are you off for summer in Devonshire? The two last days have brought ours back again – I am writing out of doors in our little arbour with my attention somewhat distracted by a superb butterfly close by who is fluttering round and round in the sun and swinging in the rich blossom of a China aster – how fond they are of China asters! So am I – They come when flowers begin to be most precious and rare – I have never had so many before or so fine – and they are always beautiful with their rich colours like so many patterns for winter gowns – or with pure delicate white stripes mingled with purple like violets of both hues – And they are so hardy too – they hold up their gay heads and *will* live, let the weather be what it may. . . .

But indeed in this little garden I have had a great crop of flowers of all sorts – It's quite astonishing how little room they will do with, and I like that crowd of bright blooms mingling one with the other like flowers in a market or the mimic gaiety of a carpet. I have been bringing in my harvest of sweet peas today.

To Sir William Elford, Bickham, Plymouth

Three Mile Cross, 16 November 1822

First, my very dear friend, let me thank you heartily and sincerely for your very kind and delightful letter. Secondly, let me pray you to thank Mr Elford and your charming daughter for two that have given me great pleasure. I do not write to them, because when I have so good a channel for conveying my thanks, it would be but troubling them. My occupation is, writing another tragedy – my amusement is, gardening. I have now in my little garden one of the most beautiful chrysanthemums ever seen – worth coming from Bickham to see, if you be a chrysanthemum fancier. It is a very large double white flower, almost as pure and splendid as the double white camelia, and has in the inside a spot larger than a shilling of the deepest, richest purple. You never saw anything more magnificent. We imagine that this extraordinary colouring must have proceeded from some of the purple plant being mixed in with the root of the white, which is in itself a very beautiful contrast; but the white, with the purple inside, is really superb. It is covered with blossoms, and excites the envy of all the gardeners and half the ladies in the neighbourhood.

Farewell. I see no company, read no books, and as Mama says, keep all my wit for the magazines.

To Miss Jephson, Castle Martyr, Ireland

Three Mile Cross, 10 July 1824

We have a pretty little pony-chaise and pony (oh! how I should like to drive you in it!), and my dear father and mother have been out in it three or four times, to my great delight; I am sure it will do them both so much good. My great amusement is in my garden (I am so glad you have a little demesne of your own too – it is a pretty thing to be queen over roses and lilies, is it not?) My nook of ground is very beautiful this year – rosy, as one of the poems in Lalla Rookh crammed with all sorts of flowers, and parted from, or joined to, the long open shed where we sit, and which Harriette and Mama call the arcade by a double row of rich rich geraniums, at which I now look without any tender fears because Mrs Reeve has promised to house them for me during the winter – a very precious piece of hospitality. By the way, Mrs Reeve, besides bringing her charming self to Whitley (the only thing that could have consoled me for the loss of our dear friends) has also imported a most valuable and faithful female servant – a warmhearted Irishwoman, who loves everybody that her mistress loves – so that with old faithful Rainer at the gate with his face of welcome, hers at the door, and her mistress's in the parlour, Whitley is quite itself again. Nevertheless, I never go to it without wishing for our dear friends. . . .

Being a good deal unhinged by the anxiety I suffered during my dear father's illness, and therefore unfit for writing (though not at all ill, and now getting the better even of that nervousness), I have been reading an immense number of books, old and new, good and indifferent. Will you have a specimen of the brief one-, two-, or three-word character with which I put them down in a catalogue which I keep of works as I read them?

Captain Hall's 'South America' (the Loo-Choo man excellent).

Landor's 'Imaginary Conversations' (very, very good – very, very bad).

'Captain Rock' (witty and tiresome – is it true?)

Charles Lamb's Works (for the third time – and that is saying enough).

'Redgauntlet' (for the first, and I fear the last).

'The Inheritance' (clever – too clever – but not genial – not amiable – written by one who sees faults too plainly by half).

'Wilhelm Meister's Apprenticeship' (Mignon a gem – the setting rather German).

'Letters to and from Lady Suffolk' (very particularly naughty – especially the maids of honour).

'Travels', I forget where – by, I forget whom – just exactly nothing at all.

Are you not glad that I come to the end of my list and my letter? – come to the thousand loves and good wishes that attend you from all here? Adieu!

from 'Doctor Tubb', *Our Village*

On taking possession of our present abode, about four years ago, we found our garden, and all the gardens of the straggling village street in which it is situated, filled, peopled, infested by a beautiful flower, which grew in such profusion, and was so difficult to keep under, that (poor pretty thing!) instead of being admired and cherished and watered and supported, as it well deserves to be, and would be if it were rare, it is disregarded, affronted, maltreated, cut down, pulled up, hoed out, like a weed. I do not know the name of this elegant plant, nor have I met with any one who does; we call it the Spicer, after an old naval officer who once inhabited the white house just above, and, according to tradition, first brought the seed from foreign parts. It is a sort of large veronica, with a profusion of white gauzy flowers streaked with red, like the apple blossom. Strangers admire it prodigiously; and so do I – everywhere but in my own garden.

I never saw anything prettier than a whole bed of these spicers, which had clothed the top of a large heap of earth belonging to our little mason by the road-side. Whether the wind had carried the light seed from his garden, or it had been thrown out in the mould, none could tell; but there grew the plants as thick and close as grass in a meadow, and covered with delicate red and white blossoms like a fairy orchard. I never passed without stopping to look at them; and, however accustomed to the work of extirpation in my own territories, I was one day half-shocked to see a man, his pockets stuffed with the plants, two huge bundles under each arm, and still tugging away root and branch. 'Poor pretty flower,' thought I, 'not even suffered to enjoy the waste by the road-side! chased from the very common of nature, where the thistle and the nettle may spread and flourish! Poor despised flower!' This devastation did not, however, as I soon found, proceed from disrespect; the spicer-gatherer being engaged in sniffing with visible satisfaction to the leaves and stalks of the plant, which (although the blossom is wholly scentless) emit when bruised a very unpleasant odour. 'It has a fine venomous smell,' quoth he in soliloquy, 'and will certainly when stilled be good for something or

other.' This was my first sight of Doctor Tubb.

We have frequently met since, and are now well acquainted, although the worthy experimentalist considers me as a rival practitioner, an interloper, and hates me accordingly. He has very little cause. My quackery – for I plead guilty to a little of that aptness to offer counsel in very plain and common cases, which those who live much among poor people, and feel an unaffected interest in their health and comfort, can hardly help – my quackery, being mostly of the cautious, preventive, safe side, common-sense order, stands no chance against the boldness and decision of his all-promising ignorance. He says, Do! I say, Do not! He deals in *stimuli*, I in sedatives; I give medicine, he gives cordial waters.

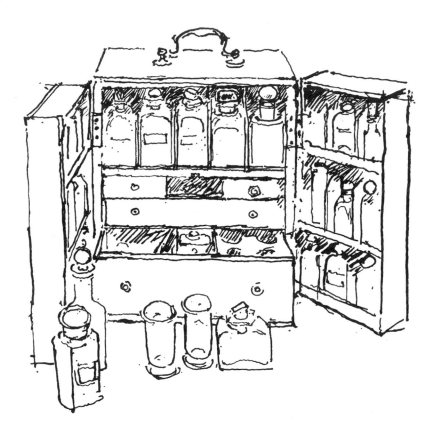

To Miss Jephson, Bath

Three Mile Cross, 27 May 1825

My dear Friend

We rejoice to hear that you are well and in England, and with friends whom you love so much – Oh how I wish you were passing near us! I have been sitting all the morning in my little garden, with its roses and stocks of all kinds, and rich peonies and geraniums, and purple irises and periwinkles, and yellow laburnums and globe anemones, and greens vivid and beautiful even as flowers, making altogether the finest piece of colour I ever saw – and I really yearned after you – you would have liked it so much. It is provoking to show such a thing to common eyes, which go peeping about into the detail, pulling the effect to pieces as children do daisies – Besides the nightingale and the scent of lilies of the valley and honeysuckles – my garden, on which my father rallies me so much, is my passion. But you will forgive me for overrating it. It is, at least, a mistake on the right side, to be too fond of one's own poor home – and no mistake at all to wish you in it.

To Miss Jephson, Hatfield, Herts

Three Mile Cross, 30 October 1829

. . . Did I tell you that it is the scarlet potentilla, which sells at fifteen shillings, being manufacturerd (I don't know how) out of the *Potentilla Formosa* and running from the colour when propagated by seed. *Our* plant, which is quite as pretty – prettier, I think – hardy and generous both in seed and root – will be an established garden flower, like pinks and roses, and always a pet with me for your sake, dearest, and for Mr Wordworth's. Don't let us forget to send you some seed from the Rydal Mount plant next season.

I have had a magnificent present of greenhouse plants, chiefly geraniums – a whole cartload – and am at present labouring under *l'embarras des richesses*, not being sure whether even the genius of Clarke will make the greenhouse hold them. *À propos* to that astrolger, I have got the ephemeris.* Marianne finding even Mrs Scott fail, took heart at last and applied to Captain Kater; who, being himself a demi-semi believer, has lent us the identical thing for our purpose, in the shape of an almanac published by order of the Board of Longitude. Between ourselves, I believe it's the identical Board of Longitude copy, from which, he says, a horoscope can be framed with the most perfect nicety and exactness. I have not seen Clarke since I obtained this treasure, but am expecting him every day.

Now, my dearest, I am going to tell you of an exploit of mine which I longed for you extremely to share. Last Saturday I dined out, and was reproached by a young fox-hunter with never having seen the hounds throw off. I said I should like the sight. The lady of the house said she would drive me some day. The conversation dropped, and I never expected to hear more of it. The next day, however, Sir John Cope (the master of the hounds)

---

*. . . I have prevailed on Clarke . . . to cast my nativity, and am going to send to our friend, the fat woman of Seven Dials, to get me an ephemeris [White's London Almanack] for the year 1787, on the 16th December, in which year, at a quarter before ten at night, I had the honour to be born . . . [Clarke] is only tempted into doing mine by the knowledge that my life has been one of vicissitudes, and will bring his science to the test.

calling on my friend, the thing was mentioned and settled; and the young man who originally suggested the matter rode over to let me know that at half-past nine the next day our friend would call for me. At half-past nine, accordingly, she came in a little limber pony-carriage drawn by a high-blooded little mare, whom she herself (the daughter and sister of a whole race of fox-hunters) had been accustomed to hunt in Wiltshire, and attended by her husband's hunting-groom excellently mounted.

The day was splendid and off we set. It was the first day of the season. The hounds were to meet in Bramshill Park, Sir John Cope's old place; and it was expected to be the greatest field and most remarkable day of many seasons; Mr Warde, the celebrated fox-hunter – the very Nestor of the field, who, after keeping foxhounds for fifty-seven years, has just, at seventy-nine, found himself growing old and given them up – was on a visit to the house, and all the hunt were likely to assemble to see this delightful person; certainly the pleasantest old man that it ever has been my fortune to foregather with – more beautiful than my father, and in the same style.

Well, off we set – got to Bramshill just as breakfast was over – saw the hounds brought out in front of the house – drove to cover – saw the fox found, and the first grand burst at his going off – followed him to another covert, and the scent being bad and the field so numerous, that he was constantly headed back, both he, who finally ran to earth, and another fox found subsequently, kept dodging about from wood to wood in that magnificent demesne – the very perfection of park scenery, hill and dale, and wood and water – and for about four hours, we with our spirited pony, kept up with the chase, driving about over road and no road, across ditches and through gaps, often run away with, sometimes almost tossed out, but with a degree of delight and enjoyment such as I never felt before, and never, I verily believe, shall feel again. The field (above a hundred horsemen, most of them the friends of my fair companion) were delighted with our sportsmanship, which in me was unexpected; they showed us the kindest attention – brought me the brush – and when, at three o'clock, we and Mr Warde and one or two others went into luncheon, whilst the hounds went on to Eversley, I really do not believe that there was a gentleman present ungratified by our gratification. Unless you have seen such a scene you can hardly imagine its animation or its beauty. The horses are most beautiful, and the dogs, although not pretty separately, are so when collected and in their own scenery; which is also exactly the case with the fox hunters' scarlet coats.

I had seen nothing of the park before, beyond the cricket-ground, and never could have had such a guide to its inmost recesses – the very heart of its sylvan solitudes – as the fox. The house – a superb structure of Elizabeth's day, in proud repair – is placed on so commanding an eminence that it seemed meeting us in every direction, and harmonized completely with the old English feeling of the park and the sport. You must see Bramshill. It is like nothing hereabouts, but reminds me of the grand Gothic castles in the north of England – Chillingham, Alnwick, &c. It was the residence of Prince Henry, James the First's eldest son, and is worthy his memory. It has a haunted room, shut up and full of armour; a chest where they say a bride hid herself on her wedding-day, and the spring-lock closing, was lost and perished, and never found until years and years had passed (this story, by-the-way, is common to old houses; it was told me of the great house at Malsanger); swarms with family pictures; has a hall with the dais; much fine tapestry; and, in short, is wanting in no point of antique dignity. The Duke of Wellington went to look at it as adjoining his own estate and suiting his station; but he unwilling, I believe, to lose the interest of so much capital, made the characteristic reply that Strathfieldsaye was good enough for the duchess, and that he saw nothing to admire at Bramshill except Sir John's pretty housekeeper. I am sure Sir John is much fitter for the master of Bramshill, with his love of cricket, his hospitality, and his fox-hounds, than the Duke with all his fame.

God bless you! Tell me when you come, and how long you stay.

Ever yours, in galloping fox-hunter's haste.

To Miss Jephson, Binfield Park

Three Mile Cross, 11 December 1829

My dearest Emily,

My horoscope turns out singularly true – one part curiously true. I have been very much entertained and interested by it, and so will you be, when our astrologer explains it to you in May in the greenhouse, for it is not easy to tell in writing, or rather it would be puzzled and long. The misfortune to my greenhouse had not occurred when you were here: the snow got into the tube or chimney, and generated a vapour intolerably thick and nauseous. We have cured the evil by a larger cap to the chimney, but the plants are greatly injured, and that is vexatious, for, till their misadventures, they continued to look as well as when you saw them. However, May will repair all evils, month of delight as it is!

To Miss Jephson, Bath

Three Mile Cross, December 1830

. . . Oh, that you could see my chrysanthemums! I have one out now unlike any I ever saw. It is the shape and size of a large honeysuckle, * and the inside filled up with tubes. Each of the petals or florets (which are they?) is, on the outside, of a deep violet colour, getting, however, paler as it approaches the end, and the inside shows itself much like the inside of a honeysuckle tube, of a shining silver white, just, in some particular lights, tinged with purple. I never saw so elegant a flower of any sort; and my jar of four kinds, golden, lemon, yellow, purple, lilac, crimson, and pink, exceeds in brilliancy any display that I ever witnessed. The brightest pot of dahlias is nothing to it. My father, who has been twice in London lately (about my American 'Children's Books' and your friend 'Inez'), says that they have nothing approaching it in splendour in the new conservatories at Covent Garden. I am prodigiously vain of my chrysanthemums, and so is Clarke.

* This, by-the-way, is the shape and size of the the tassel white, only that that flower is still more curved and curled, and all of one colour.

19 December 1830

. . . I have the sweet-scented cyclamen and the Italian narcissus (the double Italian narcissus, sweeter far than the double jonquil) blooming in pots and glasses in the parlour window, whilst my autumn flowers, chrysanthemums, roses, Michaelmas daisies (the large new late one) and salvias, blue and red, are still in full bloom. I like this junction of the seasons – this forestalling of spring and prolonging of autumn – don't you? On second thoughts, my dearest, the parlour window would be the best place for the white evening primrose. Warmth will do it no harm, so that it has light and plenty of water and a little air on mild days.

To Miss Jephson, Castle Martyr, Ireland

[Middle of November, 1831]

. . . I write to acknowledge your dear letter just received. There is another letter of mine on the road to you – or rather probably received by you before now – but I send this chiefly to enclose some anemone seed, which we are sowing today. I have a great love of those gay winter flowers, which give colours so like the lost colours in old stained glass; and I shall like you to sow some of my seed in your garden. How curiously the seed expands, opening and turning back like a frieze jacket: franks are nice conveyors of seed. Have you the great white Œnothera – almost as big as a saucer – which opens at night and is so like a cup of alabaster? If you have not, I must send you seed of that when it ripens, for it is one of my pet flowers. I'll also send some seed of a certain blue pea (Lord Anson's pea) which is just the colour of Aqua Marina – the most beautiful blue of any flower; have you that? It has a small pink mark in the centre, which adds to the beauty greatly. It is small and scentless and very rare – and very rare it always will be, because it is very shy of seed. I enclose one of the petals. No – we don't use salt. Of course our geraniums won the prizes; and one seedling especially (which I have called the 'Ion', after Mr Sergeant Talfourd's play) is said to be the finest that has been produced for many years. I enclose the leaves of one flower of that also. We have at present twelve seedlings, each of which would win a prize anywhere, and one hundred and fifty more to blow. One effect of raising seedlings is, that one ceases to care for other plants – a very vain and dangerous feeling. My friend, Mr Foster, has it to such a degree that he does not suffer any plant not raised by himself or his brother in his greenhouse; but even he condescended to ask for a cutting of 'Ion', and I shall (if possible) rear one for you. By 'if possible' I mean, if I can rear three – one for Mr Sergeant Talfourd, one for Mr Forster, and the third for your dear self.

To Miss Jephson, Castle Martyr, Ireland

Three Mile Cross, 14 December 1831

Your account of Miss Edgeworth is charming. High animal spirits are amongst the best of God's gifts. I had them once; but anxiety and loneliness have tamed them down. The highest I have ever known are Lady Croft's. They have borne her through all sorts of calamities – her husband's sad death – the death of her favourite son – comparative poverty – the marriage of her only daughter to a Frenchman living in France – every sort of trial; and still she is the gayest and most charming old lady in the world – as active in mind and body at nearly eighty as most girls of eighteen. It is always bad criticism to say there is no more to be done. Beside Sir Walter's novels, the American are a new class (I mean Cooper's and Bird's – especially the Mexican stories of Dr Bird), and so are the naval novels, for 'Roderick Random' can hardly be said to have done more than opened the vein. Oh! it is false philosophy to limit the faculties and the productions of man! As well prophesy that there should be no new flowers! If T—'s money were coming to me, I should have avaricious views of accumulating geraniums, although I have already more than I can keep; and piling chrysanthemum upon chrysanthemum, although as it is I have beaten the whole county. Don't you love that delicious flower which prolongs the season of bloom until the Roman narcissus blows, and keeps the world blossoming all the year round? My salvias have been superb this year. I planted them in the ground about the middle or towards the end of July, and took them up in October – so that we got all the growth of common ground and open air, and brought them full of bud to blow in the greenhouse. Two of them nearly reached the top of the house.

At present I am altogether immersed in music. I am writing an opera for and with Charles Parker; and you would really be diverted to find how learned I am become on the subject of choruses and double choruses and trios and septets. Very fine music carries me away more than anything – but then it must be *very* fine. Our opera will be most splendid – a real opera – all singing and recitative – blank verse of course, and rhyme for the airs, with plenty of magic – an eastern fairy tale.

To THOMAS NOON TALFOURD, London

Three Mile Cross, 10 January 1834

Mrs Cherry's receipt for salade.

> Two slices of onion very thin
> One apple
> Six chilies
> One rather large raw tomato sliced
> Half a beetroot well boiled and cold before being sliced
> Two tablespoonfuls of vinegar
> Two teaspoonfuls of salt.

I have sent you this receipt, my dear kind friend, as soon as ever I received it – I suppose both the tomato and the chilies may still be got in Covent Garden though the autumn season's the proper time for them – but I believe they keep – at all events I could not send it before I got it.

To Dr Mitford, 8 King Street, Cheapside

Three Mile Cross, 13 May 1834

. . . Ben desires me to tell you to get the Wallace and the light whip for Miss Mitford; *I*, for my part, forbid you buying anything unless you sell the play ['Charles the First'] or the copyright. Ben could only get a dozen cuttings of heart's-ease yesterday, Ratten having sold all the plants. I have had the creepers planted and the dahlias, and we have two beautiful geraniums come out, and your seedling is really superb; but I am sorry to say that the cats are more mischievous than ever. They got into the greenhouse last night – broke one of our best geraniums to pieces – tore a good deal of a night-scented stock – dragged my sofa-cover all over the floor, and danced all over the looking-glass. They have also scratched up our new border of red and blue flowers under the jessamine, and are really past bearing – particularly the white one, for I don't think the tabby would be so bad if alone. All the pets are well. The mare and Ben rolled the field yesterday, and Ben desires me to say that it looks very well.

To Dr Mitford, King Street, Cheapside

15 May 1834

. . . John and Ben are gone to the flower-show, and have taken some of our blooms to compare with those shown, and mean to bring home the names of the owners of any new geraniums, that we may try to get cuttings. So we shall know as much as if I went; I am so worried and out of sorts, that I should have had no sort of pleasure there. I have no doubt but you will do for the best. I should be content with 200*l.*– 150*l.*– 100*l.* – anything rather than risk; though I have a source of confidence in the play that no one else has; for my reliance on Mr Cathcart's acting increases rather than diminishes, which – fearful and doubtful as I am of everything else – is a great comfort. But I would gladly take 100*l.* for the tragedy nevertheless. Unless you get some money, my dear love, my going to town to spend money is absolutely out of the question. I would rather have 50*l.* down than the chance of 500*l.* for I know I shall be cheated, notwithstanding Mr Serle's [actor and dramatist] kindness.

My garden really looks divine; I never saw anything so beautiful. God bless you!

To Miss Jephson, Castle Martyr, Ireland

Three Mile Cross, 30 August 1834

A thousand thanks, dearest Emily, for your most welcome letter. I am going to answer it very inadequately, being very much tired tonight, and yet not sleepy enough to go to bed. So I sit down to talk to you purely and simply to refresh me and do me good – as the very thought of you always does. My fatigue springs from two causes – one pleasant, the other very much the reverse. I have had a levée today, as is very common with me in the summer season – people from London, or people from America, or people from Germany, or people from France; all clever, and almost all pleasant; and I became excited, and was quite done up, when we found out that some valuable geraniums, which had been stolen from our pits and advertised yesterday, had been carried away by a man only three doors off, whom we had employed for years, and done all for that our means would allow. He stole them and sold them to a neighbour, and then, finding that they were advertised, and that he should be detected, stole them again last night from the lady to whom he had sold them. Now, this is grievous. He might have had eight plants for asking, as freely as you might. This does one harm, does it not? My father is quite unhappy, but I think that I was too vain and fond of my plants, and that it is a punishment. Well, I will talk of it no more.

Did I tell you that I had called my best seedling after Mr Sergeant's play? [Talfourd's *Ion*] Yes, I did. And did I tell you that I had an autograph of Mr O'Connell's – most characteristic? Here it is:

> Still shalt thou be my waking theme,
> Thy glories still my midnight dream;
> And every thought and wish of mine,
> Unconquered Erin! shall be thine!
> Daniel O'Connell

August 4, 1834.

I was afraid that it was a regular circular autograph, but I heard of one different the other day, and have found out that this was written for me expressly, which rejoices me much. I have just been writing a sermon on Tolerance, the virtue most wanted in Ireland, on both sides, I think; you and yours, and Daniel O'Connell himself, seeming to me the only tolerant persons of your country, Protestant or Catholic.

I know your beautiful rose; it is French. I am to have that, and others, from Mr Anderdon, whose collection of roses is as choice as his collection of pictures. Do you know the Devonshire briar? It is covered with semi-double flowers, and sweeter than any flower I ever smelt – sweeter than the magnolia, the double jonquil, the tuberose – anything. There are three thousand roses with names!!! chiefly French. 'T'other day I found a golden beetle in a York and Lancaster rose, and counted above thirty glowworms in a lovely lane between our house and Mr Palmer's. Five were close together – a constellation on the grass – earthly stars, really lighting the place. This, with the bee-bird, makes out more of summer than ought to belong to this cold weather. I heard a pretty story of a bird the other day. A friend of mine at Dover left a rare Indian bird hanging in a cage by an open window. Her house on the esplanade faces the sea. On her return she found another bird of the same species perched on the top of the cage, quite tame and gentle. All inquiries after its owner failed, and they suppose that it had escaped from some vessel, having been brought over for the purpose of traffic, and had been guided by some strange instinct to the captive of its own land.

To Miss Jephson, Castle Martyr, Ireland

Three Mile Cross, 24 December 1834

Did you ever read Victor Hugo's 'Notre Dame'? *That* is, in my mind, the most extraordinary work of this age, with all its painfulness; and Victor Hugo and Daniel O'Connell are the only two persons (not friends) whom I would cross the threshold to meet. My passion for Daniel is extraordinary – fed and fostered, certainly, by some delightful Irish people who have bought our old house, Captain Edward Gore, R.N., son of the late and brother of the present Earl of Arran. The Liberator does seem to me a most wonderful person, full of power of every sort, and, I should think, very kind and genial. I certainly, the next time I go to London, will manage to get acquainted with him.

Mr Sergeant Talfourd is growing in fame and in income. They say that he makes 5000*l.* or 6000*l.* a year now, and he has refused requisitions to stand from Derby and Bridgnorth, and another offer to be brought into Parliament at no expense from a quarter which would be to him more tempting than all – his native town of Reading. But he declines at present, for fear of putting Mr Palmer to expense or endangering his seat.

My chrysanthemums have been, and many of them still are, very splendid; one especially, a small, but most rich and regular flower, called the button white, is, I really think, as beautiful a plant as blows. It is of the purest white, whiter even than the larger and looser flower called the paper white; whiter than a lily, and of singular compactness and beauty of form. Do you know it? I have six kinds of white chrysanthemums, and about seventeen varieties in all. I wonder if I could send you any slips or cuttings, or bits with roots to them, in the spring. My finest flowers have been on cuttings not taken from the plant till late in June, or early in July. Indeed, I believe that none are taken till the latter month. This is quick work, is it not? My geraniums look very promising, and I do heartily wish that you could see my garden. It has been so much altered this year, that Emma would not know it again. . . .

To MISS JEPHSON, Castle Martyr, Ireland
Three Mile Cross, 18 May 1835

I write immediately, my dearest Emily, to say that we shall avail ourselves of the knowledge that plants can reach you safely, to send three or four pots with little geraniums (last year's cuttings), and the white chrysanthemum which you have not, and which the gardeners hereabouts call the button white. I hope that it will blow well. It is to other white chrysanthemums what the little Banksia rose is to other roses – only that the colour is as pure as milk, as lilies, as snow. I have not yet quite settled what geraniums to send; of course my best, but I am not quite sure which are my best. At present I meditate sending a 'Miss Mitford', or rather one of the 'Miss Mitfords', for there are several so called; it being a pretty proof of the way in which gardeners estimate my love of flowers, that they are constantly calling plants after me, and sending me one of the first cuttings as presents. There is a dahlia now selling at ten guineas a root under my name; I have not seen the flower, but have just had one sent me (a cutting), which will of course blow in the autumn.

I have your book of 'Irishmen and Irishwomen', dearest; but I fear it would be dangerous to send that with the flowers. You must come and fetch it yourself. Yes, I know the beautiful tree peony, the lovely Indian-looking flower, so gorgeously oriental, and like the old rich Chinese paper which one sees in houses fitted up eighty years ago. What a size yours must have been! The camellias now-a-days and the rhododendrons and azaleas, and the hybrids between the rhododendrons and azaleas, are really wonderful; I have seen plants that have been sold for twenty guineas, and which to rich people are fairly worth the money. The most beautiful of either tribe that I ever saw is a large buff azalea of matchless elegance, still very rare. But, after all, I like geraniums better than anything; and it is lucky that I do, since they are comparatively easy to rear and manage, and do not lay one under any tremendous obligation to receive, for I never buy any. All my varieties (amounting to at least three hundred different sorts) have been either presents, or exchanges, or my own seedlings – chiefly exchanges; for when once one has a good collection, that becomes an easy mode of enlarging it; and it is one pleasant to all parties, for it is a very great pleasure to have a flower in a friend's garden. You, my own Emily, gave me my first plants of the potentilla, and very often as I look at them I think of you. You must send me some little seed in a letter, as a return for these plants, seeds of your own gathering and from your own garden; and it shall go hard but I will make them grow: any seed that you think pretty.

To Miss Jephson, Castle Martyr, Ireland
Three Mile Cross, 3 September 1835

. . . I send you, my dearest Emily, the four white œnotheras, the blue pea, the *Salpiglossis picta*, the white Clarkia, a new lupine, the most beautiful that I have ever seen, similar to the *Lupinus mutabilis*, in kind and fragrance, but a clear lilac and clear white, and of far larger spikes of flowers (I enclose a flower), a new annual chrysanthemum (Cape marigold) with yellow outer leaves, and two little packets of seeds from Madeira, sent me by a gentleman whom I have never either seen or even heard of till now, but who, having been ordered there for his health, took my books with him, and found them of so much amusement to him that he sent me some seeds on his arrival by way of return, and we are likely to become great friends.

20 September 1835

I take the chance, my own dear Emily, of your not having the enclosed seed. The *Polyphillus lupine* is beautiful, but not fragrant. It blows in May, bearing spikes of flowers as thick together as possible – the one sort of a bright rich purple, the other of a very pure white. We had one plant last spring, of which the spikes were above forty in number, and many of them from three quarters of a yard to a yard long. It was new ground, and a southern aspect; but it is almost always a magnificent plant, with its palm-like leaves, in the middle of which (the last stalk from which they spread) a drop of rain will stand and shine like a diamond. It is often raised by parting the roots, but we always propagate it by seed. It blows the second year constantly, and often the first; and we think it prospers better than from the root. The little blue lobelia is beautiful in masses; we have a border of it under the white jessamine at the end of the greenhouse, where it is mixed with tufts of scarlet verbena – or rather the tufts of scarlet verbena are set amongst the lobelia, and they have been for three months covered with innumerable bright flowers, and will remain so till the frost. The seeds must be sown in a pot in the hotbed early in the spring, and set out while still very small, and really their delicate strength is wonderful. The dark nasturtium is a fine colour, and very luxuriant; and the new Marvel of Peru has a long white tube, which is sweet in the open air and pretty.

I dare say you have these flowers, but I send them upon the chance. So, too, I dare say you have the white petunia (which grows better from seed than from cuttings; the purple petunia I am afraid does not seed); the Virginia flax, a pretty perennial (is not sending flax to Ireland something like sending coals to Newcastle?); and the *Hybiscus Africanus*, which is, by the way, one of my pet flowers. I know nothing more beautiful than the dark eye contrasted with the mellow, yellowish white of the sect of the petals. The moth mullein – for that is its true name – is full of seed, but it is not yet ripe; I shall certainly send you the first that is ready. It is pretty, and I love it all the better because my father is so fond of it. I wish I knew whether I have anything else you would like. I have above seventy sorts of seed done up in little packets in one of the baskets that foreign-dried fruits come in, and they look so tidy and old-maidish that I can't help laughing when I look at them. Would you like seed of the scarlet geranium? By the way, our tuberoses this year were superb; I never saw any so large, or half so large – just like flowers carved out of marble. I suppose the hot, dry weather suited them. I am to have some Madeira lily roots from Mr Blewitt. Do you know the Madeira lily? It is a species of the Belladonna, a bright pink.

To Sir William Elford, The Priory Totnes

Three Mile Cross, 20 October 1835

My Dear Friend,

One change Lady Adams [Elford's daughter] must expect in sending her eldest hope to a public school – that he who went a boy will return a man; for anything so precocious as the young gentlemen who emerge from Eton, Harrow, and Westminster (I know less of William of Wykeham's disciples) one shall seldom see on a summer's day. Nevertheless, although the change be at first a little startling, I believe that it wears away, and that the lads turn out no worse than their shy, bashful, awkward predecessors of thirty years ago.

Yes! the rose beetle is of a burnished golden green. It comes in hot summers and only in hot summers in company with tribes of glowworms and flights of small blue butterflies and death's-head moths and large green dragonflies and the thrice-beautiful *Sphinx ligustri* – or as the common people prettily call it the bee-bird. – Another characteristic of this hot dry summer has been the manner in which the large humble-bees (vulgarly dumbledoms) have forced open – torn apart – the buds of my geraniums – an operation I never saw them perform before. Another novelty of this season has been that the splendid new annual, the *Salpiglossis picta* has after the first crop of blossoms produced perfect seed without flower petals – a proof (if any were needed) that the petals which constitute the beauty of a flower are not necessary to its propagation – I am again suffering from nervous rheumatism in the face. It came on with the change of the weather first, as it did last year and I suppose that nothing but a continued residence in a hot climate (which is out of the question with me) would remove it. – My father, I thank Heaven, is well and joins me in kindest regards to all near Totnes.

To Miss Jephson, Castle Martyr, Ireland

Three Mile Cross, 29 April 1836

Yes, my dear love, the anemones are doubtless mine, for mine of the same seed sown at the same time are in full bloom. They are hardly red enough to please me, for I like them to be of the brightest colours, and most of mine are pale, of very pretty shades, pink and lilac and white, and some red and crimson, and many purple; but not the blaze of scarlet that I like in anemones. I want them to look like an old window of stained glass, or like my own geraniums in their summer glow, for there is nothing so bright as they are – except in the garden of Aladdin, where the blossoms were of rubies and amethysts – and so you would say if you saw them in June.

By the way, there is a most beautiful poem on the blue anemone in poor Mrs Hemans's posthumous volume, which I have just received from her sister, Mrs Hughes (the composer of the 'Captive Knight', and other songs of hers), together with a very interesting letter. On her dying bed Mrs Hemans used to recur to my descriptions of natural scenery, and meant if she had lived to have inscribed to me a volume of prose recollections, which she intended to have published. This would have been a very high honour; but perhaps there is a quiet, sad, serene, gratification in the private consciousness of such an intention, even more gratifying than the public distinction, and certainly more pure.

To Miss Barrett, Gloucester Place

Three Mile Cross, 16 August 1836

My Dear Friend,

Did Henry Chorley call himself? He told me that his heart had failed him. The nosegay was a very shabby one* – I was myself in all the grief of parting from this same Henry Chorley, one of the most affable companions I have ever known, and I was besides *befraddled* by the eternal visitors, morning and evening visitors, who make this cottage during the summer and autumn months a sort of tea-garden, or rural Beulah Spa – then, John, the lad who manages my geraniums, was, on his part, in the joyful agony of preparing for the Reading Horticultural Show. For my own part, my vanity goes rather to the beauty of the flowers in a mass, or in that great nosegay my garden, than to the mere points of growth, and bloom, and sorts, by which the judges at flower-shows decide their merit. Nevertheless, as John loves to get prizes, and I have no objection, why we take the thing in very good part; only it certainly (joined with my grief at losing a pet visitor) spoilt your posy; at least made that shabby which ought to have been splendid.

* . . . After all your depreciation of the flowers, I persist in admiring them, – and should, in the very presence of the crowned John. . . . [I] shall *deduce* the beauty of the prized from the beauty of the depreciated. If this is your dust, what must your stars be? And so you must look very disdainfully on the praises of my ignorance; and that you may not, I shall try to keep out of sight as long as I can the details of it – and never tell you quite plainly how little I know one sort of geraunium [sic] from another by its name – not even when John is out of the way.

Elizabeth Barrett

To Miss Barrett, Gloucester Place

Three Mile Cross, 4 May 1837

A thousand thanks, my dear friend, for your kind inquiries after Dash. He is quite well again, better and younger than he has been for months, or even years. Yesterday he ran at least twenty miles, having accompanied my father and myself in a flowering expedition to Penge Wood for the delicate wood-sorrel and other wood flowers, and to the Kennett Meadows for the white and speckled fritillary and other meadow blossoms. By the way, is it not an extraordinary thing that the blackthorn (sloe blossom) is just coming into bloom in the hedges and the fritillary is in bloom in the meadows; the one being a blossom (as you well know) of March, early March; the other seldom out until the middle of May, along with its cousins the tulips? Well, we went on this expedition in a pony phaeton, leaving it at the wood and the meadows, and wallking about there and gathering flowers so that of some ten miles we contrived to make a four hours' ride, and Dash ran away four several times, beguiled by hares and so forth, and had a *démêlé*, which I should like you to have seen and heard, with a huge hedgehog, whose passive resistance was too much for my poor pet, but which we brought home in a basket, and put into the kitchen garden, where there is a hedge and water, and from which if he should choose to run away he can. I think he won't for he was very sociable in coming home, and as we put milk in his way, and shall continue to do so, I expect him to remain in that state of semi-tameness, which, in the country, is what I like best to see in birds or wild animals, protected but not confined. My love to your doves. How I wish the eggs would be good! It would be such a delight to you to help the parent birds to bring up their young. I told the story of the bird's nest-making to my young artist Edmund Havell, and he said, 'What a picture!' If he painted faces as well as he paints animals, I am sure that he would try.

So far as I can find, the people who call themselves scientific never chance upon useful inventions, and the objects that they pursue are as devoid of use

as they are of beauty. Moreover, they are themselves, for the most part, so scornful and conceited that we are at perfect liberty to 'scorn the scorner'. Only think, for instance, of botanists, who know no more of the cultivation of a plant than the desk I am writing on, despising florists and horticulturists, who bring the lovely flowers and the goodly thing, fruit, to such perfection! And they can't even agree about their own jargon! We had the other day a pitched battle in my garden between a set of Linnaeans and a set of Jussicuans. Oh! if you had heard the clatter! I was fain to bring forth my own list of new annuals (I have sixty, most of which have never blown in England), and had the glory of out-long-wording both parties, to the shame of floriculture, who ought to speak plain. I wish you had been present; it was a curious scene. The best stroke at science which I have met with for a long time is in the last 'Pickwick'. I hope you love humour; I, for my part, delight in it, and hold Mr Dickens to be the next great benefactor of the age to Sir Walter Scott. There is about him, too, an anti-cant and anti-humbug spirit which is worth anything.

My book is called 'Country Stories'. It is passing slowly through the press, and will not, I suppose, be advertised till nearly ready. I speak the real truth in saying that I do not like it. If ever I did like any of my prose works it was 'Belford Regis', and this is more in the way of 'Our Village'. Mr Browning seems studiously to have thrown poetry aside in his tragedy, as Shelley did; though I doubt if his subject can be so dramatic as the horribly powerful story of the 'Cenci'.

And now, my ever-dear love, Heaven bless you! We are going flowering again, to a copse full of primroses and ground ivy, and wood anemones. I wish you were with us!

To the REVD WILLIAM HARNESS, Heathcote Street

Three Mile Cross, 1 October 1837

MY DEAR FRIEND,

I have been very unwell during the greater part of this summer, for two months never past the outer door, and now that I am pretty well again we are in great trouble. Our landlady, who is a most singular compound of miser and shrew, refuses to put this poor cottage, where we have lived for seventeen years without having one shilling laid out by the owner, into the decent repair without which a great part of it will fall upon our heads, so that we are compelled to move.

Luckily, a comfortable roomy farmhouse, about half a mile off, is vacant, the farmer who rents the land living at another farm; and we may have this at thirty pounds a year, he, the farmer, paying the rates, taxes, &c., and we having a meadow of three acres into the bargain. But the garden is a potato-ground, and I am heart-broken at leaving my flowers, and frightened to death at the expense of moving and making a garden; for we having the materials, my father insists upon transporting them to our new abode; and certainly it will be less expensive to make the garden there than to do all that must be done to this poor cabin, which I love dearly in spite of all its deficiencies and faults. Still it will be a great expense, and I shall never like the new house as I do the old.

I must tell you a pretty thing that has happened close by. The journeyman of our neighbour the shoe-maker has caught my love of flowers, and having borrowed of his brother the blacksmith a little bit of waste ground by the forge, behind some poplars which draw all the nourishment from the earth, so that they could not raise cabbages there, planted it with seedling dahlias (about two hundred), which he used to water night and morning all the summer with a *can*, which he carried backward and forward from the pond at the top of the street. Well, he has got the best seedling of the year, the very best. It happened to be in bloom in time for the last Reading show; gained, of course, the cottagers' prize, and he will get something between 5*l* and 10*l*. for the root, besides the honour. I never, I think, saw such a happy face in my life as his at the flower show. He never stirred from his flower. All the gardeners far and near (for it was a grand dahlia show open to all England, and we had twelve prizes for strangers, and they came from beyond London) clustered about him; and John Brown and his dahlia were the lions of the day. I think I enjoyed it as much as he did; his love of flowers was so genuine, and his success so entirely deserved.

A dear friend of mine, who is appointed superintendent of the Queen's dressers, gives a very interesting account of her. She says she is a girl of great power, sedate and serious far beyond her years, and fully equal to all that she will be required to do. . . .

To Miss Jephson, Bath

Three Mile Cross, 4 July 1838

. . . Did I tell you that we have a very pretty little brown spaniel? He was Ben's. A year ago a savage boy broke his poor little leg. We nursed him and cured him, and he stayed about the place, and now he has crept in by degrees, and is a most loving and amusing little creature, with the most beautiful short shiny curly coat that can be. My father is very fond of him indeed. I have been offered dogs of all sorts, but we could not be better off than with poor little Flush (that is his name, Flush) unless we could get such another as my lamented and noble Dash. It is one of Flush's recommendations that he was very, very fond of dear, dear Dash, and that our noble and gracious pet liked him. Indeed, I don't believe that my father would now change Flush for any dog.

My present passion is for indigenous orchises. I had a good collection last year, but they were trampled under foot during the winter, when I was too ill to attend to them. I have now one or two specimens only of the bee orchis, and several of the butterfly, which is the most exquisitely fragrant of the night-scented plants. If I could get about amongst the Oxfordshire woods I could enlarge my collection, but, as it is, I am obliged to trust to the kindness of friends, having only been able to make one excursion to get the butterfly orchises. Your convolvulus major is in great beauty, so are my geraniums, and a certain exquisite carmine pea; also a delicate white pea, freaked in blue and pink, a most unusual union of colour, quite like old china. You will be glad to hear that the bay tree is coming up strong from the roots at one part, better than if from several, and we shall be magnificent in dahlias, having one hundred and eight of the very finest known. Oh, if you could but come to see us!

To Miss Barnett, Torquay

Three Mile Cross, 28 June 1841

First, my beloved friend, let me answer your most kind inquiries. I am greatly better. It has been a most remarkable escape; but a real escape. I cannot yet turn in my bed; but when up I get about astonishingly well. To say truth, I am, and always have been, a very active person – country-born and country-bred – with great fearlessness and safety of foot and limb. Ever *since* this misfortune, Ben having said that half the parish had mounted on a hayrick close by to look at the garden, which lies beneath it (an acre of flowers rich in colour as a painter's palette), I could not resist the sight of the ladder, and one evening when all the men were away, climbed up to take myself a view of my flowery domain. I wish you could see it! Masses of the Siberian larkspur, and sweet Williams, mostly double, the still brighter new larkspur (*Delphinium Chinensis*), rich as an oriental butterfly – such a size and such a blue! amongst roses in millions, with the blue and white Canterbury bells (also double), and the white foxglove, and the variegated monkshood, the carmine pea, in its stalwart beauty, the nemophila, like the sky above its head, the new chrysanthemum, with its gay orange tufts, hundreds of lesser annuals, and fuchsias, zinnias, salvias, geraniums past compt; so bright are the flowers that the green really does not predominate amongst them!

Yes! I knew you would like those old houses! Orkwells surpasses in beauty and in preservation anything I ever saw. Our ancestors were rare architects. Their painted glass and their carved oak are unequalled.

To the REVD WILLIAM HARNESS, Heathcote Street

Three Mile Cross, 22 July 1841

This has been a summer of extraordinary escapes. Six weeks back I was dragged by a friend, who was handing me over the rafters in an unfloored room, across the joists, a depth of four feet and a half – a terrible jar upon the spine, which I have only just recovered; and two nights ago I was writing with a low candle by the side of the desk when the frill of my nightcap (the edging of the border) took fire. I saw and felt the flames. Everybody was in bed and asleep. My hands trembled so that I could not undo the strings of the cap, and I flung myself upon the ground and extinguished it with the hearthrug; frightening nobody except poor dear little Flush, who was asleep on my father's chair, but (roused I suppose by the smell of fire) sate up, with his beautiful eyes dilated to three times their usual size fixed upon me, shaking as if in an ague, and whining with distress. He nearly devoured me with caresses when I went to him. My head was a good deal scorched (it was a very startling sensation to see and feel the flames), but the immediate application of Goulard prevented any mischief; and I am so thankful not to have alarmed my father or indeed any one.

To Miss Barrett, Wimpole Street

Three Mile Cross, 27 April 1842

. . . No! my dear love, I am not now about to write on the subject of the
South Seas. The first volume of any size that I printed was on the story –
which came to me from a friend of the American captain who visited them –
of Christian's Colony on Pitcairn's Island. A large edition was sold. Then I
published a second edition of a volume of miscellaneous poems; then another
volume of narrative poems called 'Blanch and the Rival Sisters'. All sold
well, and might have been reprinted; but I had (of this proof of tolerable taste
I am rather proud) the sense to see that they were good for nothing, so that I
left off writing for twelve or fifteen years, and should never have committed
any more pen-and-ink sins, had not our circumstances become such as to
render the very humblest exertions right. My dear mother's health was then
almost what my father's is now; only then we were three, so that, except by
staying at home, I was not so absolutely chained as I am now.

Well, perhaps if I could be all the time I covet, among the sweet flowers
and the fresh grass, I should not enjoy as I do the brief intervals into which I
do contrive to concentrate so much childish felicity. Who is it that talks of
the 'the cowslip vales of England'? is it you, my beloved? The words are most
true and most dear. Oh! how I love those meadows, yellow with cowslips and
primroses; those winding brooks, or rather *that* winding brook, golden with
the water ranunculus; those Silchester coppices, clothed with wood-sorrel,
wood-anemone, wild hyacinth, and primroses in clusters as large as the table
at which I write! I do not love musk – almost the only odour called sweet that
I do not love; yet coming this evening on the night-scented odora with its
beautiful green cups, I almost loved the scent for the form on which it grew.
But the cowslips, the wild hyacinths, the primroses, the violet – oh, what
scent may match with theirs? I try to like the garden, but my heart is in the
fields and woods. I have been in the meadows tonight – I ran away, leaving
my father asleep – I could not help it. And oh! what a three hours of
enjoyment we had, Flush, and the puppies, and I! I myself, I verily believe,
the youngest-hearted of all. Then I have been to Silchester too. My father

went there; and I got out and ran round the walls and coppices one way, as he drove the other. How grateful I am to that great gracious Providence who makes the most intense enjoyment the cheapest and commonest! I do love the woods and fields! Oh! surely all the stars under the sun, even if they were brighter than those earthly stars ever seem to me, could not compare with the green grass and the sweet flowers of this delicious season!

I mistrust the feeling of poetry of all those who consent to pass the spring amongst brick walls, when they might come and saunter amongst lanes and coppices. To live in the country is, in my mind, to bring the poetry of Nature home to the eyes and the heart. And how can those who do love the country talk of autumn as rivalling the beauty of spring? Only look at the texture of the young leaves; see the sap mounting into the transparent twigs as you stand under an oak; feel the delicious buds; inhale the fragrance of bough and herb, of leaf and flower; listen to the birds and the happy insects; feel the fresh balmy air! This is a rhapsody; but I have no one to whom to talk, for if I mention it to my father, he talks of 'my killing myself', as if that which is balm and renovation were poison and suicide.

To Miss Barrett, Wimpole Street

Three Mile Cross, 20 June 1842

My dear Love,

It is now half-past one, and my father has only this very moment gone into his room to bed. He sleeps all the afternoon in the garden, and then would sit up all night to be read to. I have now several letters to answer before going to bed. At present, I write to say that on Saturday next (the very day on which you will receive this) we shall send you some flowers. Oh, how I wish we could transport you into the garden where they grow! You would like it – the '*entourage*', as Mrs Mackie calls it, is so pretty: one side (it is nearly an acre of show flowers) a high hedge of hawthorn, with giant trees rising above it beyond the hedge, whilst all down within the garden are clumps of matchless hollyhocks and splendid dahlias; the top of the garden being shut in by the old irregular cottage, with its dark brickwork covered with vines and roses, and its picturesque chimneys mingling with the bay tree, again rising into its bright and shining cone, and two old pear trees festooned with honeysuckle; the bottom of the garden and the remaining side consisting of lower hedgerows melting into wooded uplands, dotted with white cottages and patches of common. Nothing can well be imagined more beautiful than this little bit of ground is now. Huge masses of lupines (say fifty or sixty spiral spikes), some white, some lilac; immense clumps of the enamelled Siberian larkspur, glittering like some enormous Chinese jar; the white and azure blossoms of the variegated monkshood; flags of all colours; roses of every shade, some covering the house and stables and overtopping the roofs, others mingling with tall apple trees, others again (especially the beautiful double Scotch rose) low but broad, standing in bright relief to the blues and purples; and the oriental poppy, like an orange lamp (for it really seeems to have light within it) shining amidst the deeper greens; above all, the pyramid of geraniums, beautiful beyond all beauty, rising in front of our garden room, whilst each corner is filled with the same beautiful flower, and the whole air perfumed by the delicious honeysuckle. Nothing can be more lovely.

To Miss Barrett, Wimpole Street

Three Mile Cross, 25 June 1842

. . . I wonder, my very dearest, when I shall be quiet again! Last Monday I set forth to get a flower of the buck-bean. I had set my heart upon it. Whole beds of that rare plant grow upon either side of a stream that runs amongst Mr Tyshe Palmer's plantations, crossed by two bridges, called Kingsbridge and Queensbridge, on two roads which diverge so, about four miles from the little town of Wokingham. Now, Wokingham is eight miles from us; but, by crossing the heath, we save about two, at the expense of walking those two miles under the firs – a delicious walk in these balmy summer evenings, when the scent is as of Arabia. Well, I had been three times to this Kingsbridge in chase of this flower – twice, quite in vain; but the third time we had found the plant, its buds and leaves in profusion, so that I was determined not to give up the flower. Accordingly, Ben being busy finishing the hay, Marianne (my hysterical maid), and I, set forth, with the pony and Flush for all our company. The road is exquisite – by Aborfield first, and through delicious lanes walled with honeysuckle-hedges, and cradled above with beech and oak and elm – over the Lodden, with its floating water-lilies – then through the still wilder lanes and woodlands of Barkham, until we reached the heath, pink and purple with the flowers from which it takes its name – and then Mr Tyshe Palmer's exquisite plantations of fir, and larch, and beech, and mountain ash.

The name of the road we took will tell you the extent of these plantations – 'The Nine Mile Ride'; but of their beauty, diversified by little valleys with wandering brooks, and varied by the most sudden rise and fall of the ground, by bits of wild road hollowed out of the hill-side, and overgrown by shaggy precipices, and of the exquisite odours of the pines and the heath-flowers of a thousand sorts, I can give you no notion. For the last two miles we had to lead the pony, because this Nine Mile Ride may be a ride, but is no road for a wheeled vehicle. That we did not mind. We did, however, begin to fret when, on reaching the streamlet where the buck-bean grew, and traversing it on either side for above an hour, we found thousands, millions of plants, but not one blossom – most carefully had they been cut off! Ben says 'mowed'; I rather think cut by people employed by the London druggists, it being a celebrated remedy for erysipelas. However that may be, gone it was, and we had no other consolation than that of finding in profusion the equally rare bog asphodel. Do you know *that* pretty wild flower? Wet high above our boots (for we had traversed miles of bog), we prepared to set off on our way home, when a tremendous roll of thunder over our heads gave token of what was about to ensue. The pony curvetted; Flush was uneasy; hail and rain poured down in torrents – hail such as in my life I never saw; in fact, it broke all the glass it came near. In fewer minutes than I care to say we were wet to the skin; the bottom of the pony-chaise was as full of water as a bucket, and the pony was so frightened, it was clear that the best we could do was to lead it home. This we did, not meeting a creature till we got to Aborfield, by which time we had made up our minds to follow out the adventure. At first we were violently angry to be so deserted, and said to one another, rather oftener than was quite magnanimous, 'Well, if K— had been out in this rain, we should have sent after *her*! Thank Heaven, we never deserted anybody in such a manner!' But by the time we had passed Barkham we began to perceive by the state of the roads how completely local the storm had been; in fact we were, I really believe, completely in the centre both of the lightning and the hail and rain.

Never was such a plight as ours. It has spoilt my two cloaks (one a fur one – a real loss), which had been hung over the back of the chaise, and which we abandoned, as adding to the weight of water which we had to carry; but beyond this misfortune, which I shall feel severely in the winter (I must try to buy one second-hand), we escaped wonderfully. I suppose we should have been very stiff the next day if we had had time; but on Tuesday that gander feast, the Reading Whist Club, dined with us; and then, between helping to cook, and talking and waiting upon the good folks, we got the stiffness rubbed out of our bones in a wonderful manner.

To Miss Barrett, Wimpole Street

Three Mile Cross, 18 March 1845

Oh! my very dear love, I grieve that, as I had feared, you are suffering from this weather. It cannot last long, indeed I think that it is breaking already. I have had a present of some roses blown in a hothouse – cut flowers. Yesterday morning they were found on the drawing-room table, with their stalks in ice, instead of water. All the contents of the vase was frozen into a solid mass; and that in a room with a fire every day, on the 17th of March! Poor pretty roses! They did not mind it at all, and looked just as fresh and smelt as sweet as in their native conservatory. It was a strange contrast, to look at the green stalks crowned with such splendid blossoms and fixed into a mass of solid ice – summer and winter in one's hand at once. But the ice melted and the roses remained; and that is an emblem of what we may hope for now. There is comfort in that thought. My poor Flush suffers much from the weather. He has had a bad cough; and now that that is gone he has had a frightful attack of cramp from the cold. I was obliged to get him carried to Mrs Amott's, for he could not walk; and, in her warm room, in about an hour he so far recovered as to walk home. But, poor love, he has been very, very poorly and will hardly get out.

I have the first volume of Victor Hugo's 'Odes et Ballades', but they are slavishly loyal to those vile old Bourbons. What could he see in them? I suppose I shall like the second volume better.

To Miss Jephson, Castle Martyr, Ireland

Three Mile Cross, Autumn 1845

My dear Love,

Your dear letter found me after a three weeks' confinement from sickness every night, and the most acute pain in the lower limbs. Mr May says that the terrible pain, which is just like tic doloureux, in the knee-joints, *is* a pressure upon some nerve; but I cannot get rid of the fear that it is rheumatic, and that I may, some day or other lose the use of my limbs, and go about like those poor cripples in Bath, dragged along in tall chairs, looking to me the very emblems of misery. I can't help quoting Shakespeare's 'cold sciatica'; for the pain only yields to dry heat, actual washing in front of the fire, and the flesh is often as cold as marble, while the perspiration is pouring over the limb. Today, however, I am a little better, and have crept into the garden to look at my dahlias. One of my seedlings is so fine that we have sold it for twenty pounds, the highest price given for a dahlia this year. Are we not lucky to have so good a dahlia? I don't know what the nursery man (Mr Bragge of Slough) means to call it. It is white, of the most exquisite shape and cleanness, tipped with puce colour. We have some very fine seedlings *this* year, and our great bed is also full of fine old dahlias – I mean those raised by other growers; for I don't believe that we have one more than three years old, except the old Springfield, which I insist upon keeping for 'auld lang syne'. It seems to me quite grievous to throw away our ancient favourites in flowers; still it is what must be done, to keep pace with the collections round.

We have only twenty-four new seedling geraniums, having given our cast-off seedlings chiefly to nurserymen for sale, in exchange for pots and new plants of other sorts – not one past three years old even of theirs, and not one raised by any other grower. This looks like great boasting, but you must come and see next year. In the meanwhile, this twenty pounds, besides the credit, will pay for glass and coals (Ben does the glazing and carpentering and blacksmith's work all himself, as well as the painting), and justify me to

myself for my only extravagance – my dear flowers. What should I, who have only Flush to love me, and poor Ben and K—, and K—'s little boy, do without flowers? Ah! dearest Emily, I often think that of all the goodness of God, as shown to us in this beautiful world, that little world of flowers is, in its sweetness and innocence and peace, the truest and best example of what we ought to try to be ourselves; opening our hearts, as best we may, to the bright sunshine and the pure air of heaven; and sweetening and beautifying, to our fellow-creatures, the path of life along which we dwell.

No, my dear, that iris is not the fleur-de-lis, nor anything like it. It is a pretty but not rare iris; whereas the real fleur-de-lis is very rare indeed. It is of that class popularly called the flag iris, above six feet high and two or three times as large – I mean the flower. I suspect the plant to be semi-aquatic. Its having blown in two gardens after this wet spring – in one of which it had been for twelve years, in the other for twenty – without flowering, looks like it, does it not? These two are the only ones I know. The lower petal of the true flower is much more opaque, with a large oval golden spot, like ivory inlaid with gold and surrounded with alabaster.

To Miss Jephson, Castle Martyr, Ireland

Three Mile Cross, July 1846

My dear Emily,

I am sincerely rejoiced to hear that you have not suffered so much as I feared from the hot weather. It disagreed exceedingly with me; but, nevertheless, I contrived to walk through it, although the dust and the unmitigated glare were most painful and trying. My roses were blighted, my annuals dried off, and my geraniums have flagged and fallen under the glare in a most miserable manner. The peas, too, lasted only four or five days; and, in short, all vegetation has suffered. The rhododendrons at Whiteknights and at Bear-

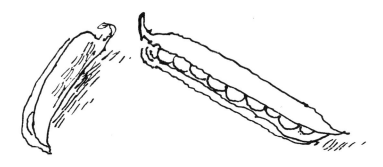

wood I never saw so fine, and my strawberries have prospered; but the currants are blighted, and they say there are in this county no apples at all.

I have been shocked past expression by the death of poor Haydon. He had sent me a ticket for a private view of his pictures only a month or two back; and we had been friends and correspondents for above thirty years. Poor fellow! He was a most brilliant person, and deserved a better fate, although he never quite kept the promise of his earlier works – never, indeed, brought out anything so really fine as the 'Judgment of Solomon' which my friend Sir William Elford purchased for six hundred pounds; and which first brought him into notice. Sir Robert Peel's conduct on this occasion has been very noble.

To Mrs Jennings

Three Mile Cross, 16 April 1850

Yes! dearest Mrs Jennings, there certainly is a sympathy, I have remarked it a hundred times, and I think our writing just at one time proves its completely. I do trust that it will lead me to London before you leave it. In other words, I constantly hope that we may meet this spring; but my coming is still uncertain, and depends upon half a dozen small circumstances over which I have myself no control. First of all, my poor cottage is falling about my ears. We were compelled to move my little pony from his stable to the chaise-house, because there were in the stable three large holes big enough for me to escape through. Then came a windy night and blew the roof from the chaise-house. And truly the cottage proper, where we two-legged creatures dwell, is in little better condition; the walls seem to be mouldering from the bottom, crumbling, as it were, like an old cheese; and, whether anything can be done with it, is doubtful. Besides which, as it belongs to chancery wards, there is a further doubt whether the Master will do what may be done.

I only want a cottage with a good bedroom, a decent sitting-room, and perhaps two odd rooms, anywhere, for books; for I find, upon taking stock, that I shall have from five thousand to six thousand. All these are reasons against going far; and, indeed, there is a cottage here which, if I can take, I shall.

To Mrs Browning, Florence, Italy

Three Mile Cross, 1 July 1850

I cannot enough thank you, my beloved friend, for your most welcome letter. The pleasure it gave me would have been unmingled but for its delaying the hope of seeing you. But, if you come so near as France, then we shall meet here, I hope, and there – I mean both in France and in England; for I do still hope to get as far as Paris before I die. At present I cannot tell you where I am going. The cottage at Swallowfield that I want to rent, belonged to a crotchetty old bachelor; he, dying, left it for her life to a sister, a rich widow, aged seventy-seven, and after her death to another relative. It is about six miles from Reading, on this same road, leading up from which is a short ascending lane, terminated by this small dwelling, with a court in front, and a garden and paddock behind. Trees overarch it like the frame of a picture, and the cottage itself, although not pretty, yet too unpretending to be vulgar, and abundantly snug and comfortable, leading by different paths to all my favourite walks, and still within distance of my most valuable neighbours. It will be provoking if this woman, who has known me for forty years, and to whom my father rendered a thousand services, should, from spite to Captain Beauchamp and his excellent father, resolve rather to let the cottage tumble to pieces than admit a tenant whom they wish to see there, or indeed any tenant at all.

You are most kind in your inquiries about my health. I cannot but think myself better on the whole than when I wrote last, and you will wonder to hear that I have again taken pen in hand. It reminds me of Benedick's speech – 'When I said I should die a bachelor, I never thought to live to be married'; but it is our friend Henry Chorley's fault. He has taken to 'The Lady's Companion', a weekly journal, belonging to Bradbury and Evans, that was going to decay (like my dwellings, present and future) under the mismanagement of Mrs Loudon, and came to me to help him. He wanted a novel; then, finding that out of the question, he wanted something else; and, though I have refused every applicant to right and left for these eight years, this very Mrs Loudon included, and began of course, by refusing him, he is such a very old friend, that I really could not persist in saying No to him. So at last it ended in my undertaking to give him a series of papers to be called 'Readings of Poetry, Old and New', consisting of as much prose as he can get, and extracts from favourite poets.

To Mrs Jennings, Portland Place

Three Mile Cross, 9 November 1850

Your two delightful letters, my very dear Mrs Jennings, deserve a better return than they are likely to get at this moment. Nevertheless, I cannot put off writing any longer. When the days get a little longer – that is to say, early in the new year – I shall do by you what I used to by Elizabeth Barrett – take a return ticket to go up for the day to Portland Place, arriving about three o'clock, or two perhaps, and returning by the half-past seven o'clock train. Then we can have a grand discussion upon a Welsh cottage. You and Mr Jennings are the temptations; the distance, and absence of books, the objections. But we must meet and have a long talk. Are there dry winter walks? that is a great point. I live entirely, I may say, on boiled sole, boiled whiting, and fruit; fish of any other sort I could not touch. And fruit – strawberries, for instance, currants, grapes – must be come-at-able, in large quantities and for a long time. We have now out-of-door grapes hung up to last till March. This, dear friend, is a point of health with me. I never can eat meat or butter, or milk or eggs, or poultry. Is there good *brown* bread? All these questions we can discuss, and I mention them now that you may ask. But I dread the want of books; I have the habit of running over almost every book of any note that is published; and a book club always has seemed to me a sort of mental imprisonment – a shutting into one little room, and being kept on water gruel. Then I have five thousand or six thousand volumes to move, as well as furniture. About neighbours I do not care. Mr Jennings and you, and one clever man, would do. I rather dislike neighbours – don't you? Do you remember what Horace Walpole says of the country? – 'Questions grow there, and the Christian commodity neighbours'. That has always seemed to me among the raciest of his racy bits. You and Mr Jennings are the temptation. And then, this cottage is likely to fall about my ears; yet I cling to it – to the green lanes – which you have not seen – to the commons, the copses, the old trees – every bit of the old country. It is only a person brought up in the midst of woods and fields, in one country place, who can understand that strong local attachment. But we must talk over the matter; most assuredly nothing but illness shall prevent my having the great pleasure of going to see you in London. You must thank for me your pleasant friend. I am ashamed not to recollect him; but that Manor House has had so many guests, that one gets confounded amongst them. Was he a visitor of Sir William Pym?

Just now, I have been much interested by a painting that has been going on in the corner of our village street – the inside of an old wheelwright's shop – a large barn-like place, open to the roof, full of detail, with the light admitted through the half of hatch doors, and spreading upwards. It is a fine subject, and finely treated. The artist is one, not yet much known, of the name of Pasmore. But I judge by this he will make a name for interiors. It is capitally peopled, too – with children, picking up chips and watching an old man sharpening a saw, and peeping in through windows, stretching up to look through them. I hear it has pleased Henry Phillips, the bass singer, to make one of his pleasant musical entertainments out of my book – for the libretto is as much his as the music – and accordingly he is coming to sing and recite 'Our Village', and I am going to hear him. Have you read 'Alton Locke'? I have not; nor, although he is almost a neighbour, do I know Mr Kingsley. His other work, 'The Saint's Tragedy', was full of power, but painful, disagreeable, and inconclusive; and I think it likely, from all that I hear, that this is the same; although my friend Mr Pearson, the vicar of Sonning, said to me yesterday that there was in it a startling amount of world-wide truth.

To Mrs Acton Tindal

Swallowfield, 3 October 1851

I am so sorry not to have seen you and your dear sister, my beloved friend, but you must come on your return, and let me know the day and the hour, and stay as long as you can. K— tells me you most kindly proposed sending me some creeping roses, and so forth – the smallest donations will be welcome for our old plants were too big to move, and we have no new ones. This place will be very comfortable by and by. It is a liveable place, wanting a pretty sitting-room but rich in all else – and the walks and drives behind, the woody lanes and pastoral water meadows of the valley of the Loddon are charming. I have a terrible job before me in arranging my books. The man who brought my things says that there were above four tons, bound and unbound. I have another terrible job in progress, finishing my own work. The friend with whom I left powers to dispose of it, sold three volumes instead of two, so I have one more to write. It will be called 'Recollections of Books' and will be almost an autobiography – I hope you will like it.

from *Recollections of a Literary Life*

. . . My most kind friend, Mr Ruskin, will understand why I connect his name with the latest event that has befallen me, the leaving the cottage that for thirty years had been my shelter. In truth, it was leaving me. All above the foundation seemed mouldering, like an old cheese, with damp and rottenness. The rain came dripping through the roof and steaming through the walls. The hailstones pattered upon my bed, through the casements, and the small panes rattled and fell to pieces every high wind . . . I found myself dragging off the skirting-board by no stronger a compulsion than the flounce of a muslin gown. The poor cottage was crumbling around us, and if we had staid much longer we should have been buried in the ruins.

And yet it was great grief to go. Besides my hatred of all change, especially change of place, a tendency to take root where I am planted, and to eschew all fresh dwellings, which renders me quite an anachronism in this loco-motive age; besides my general aversion to new habitations, I had associa-tions with those old walls which endeared them to me more than I can tell. There I had toiled and striven, and tasted as deeply of bitter anxiety, of fear, and of hope as often falls to the lot of woman. There, in the fulness of age, I had lost those whose love had made my home sweet and precious. Alas! there is no hearth so humble but it has known such tales of joy and of sorrow!

Other recollections, less dear and less sad, added their interest to the place. Friends, many and kind; strangers, whose mere names were an honour, had come to that bright garden, and that garden room. The list would fill more pages than I have to give. There Mr Justice Talfourd had brought the delightful gaiety of his brilliant youth, and poor Haydon had talked more vivid pictures then he ever painted. . . . It was a heart-tug to leave that garden.

But necessity (may I not rather say Providence?) works for us better than our own vain wishes. I did move – I was compelled to move from the dear old house; not very far; not much farther than Cowper when he migrated from Olney to Weston, and with quite as happy an effect. I walked from the one cottage to the other on an autumn evening, when the vagrant birds, whose habit of assembling here for their annual departure, gives, I suppose, its name of Swallowfield to the village, were circling and twittering over my head . . .

Here I am in this prettiest village, in the snuggest and cosiest of all snug cabins; a trim cottage garden, divided by a hawthorn hedge from a little field guarded by grand old trees; a cheerful glimpse of the high-road in front, just to hint that there is such a thing as the peopled world; and on either side the deep silent woody lanes that form the distinctive character of English scenery.

To Mrs Acton Tindal

Swallowfield, 4 February 1852

Your roses puzzled me more than I can tell. I have three or four friends in
Hertfordshire, all likely enough to have sent them; and not expecting yours
to come from that quarter, I really thought the Derings or the Jays must have
sent them. However I would rather have them from you: I shall value them
all the more as token flowers, like you in brightness and sweetness. I like
them none the less for their Bonapartist names – Souvenir de Malmaison,
Eugene Beauharnais, Géant des Batailles. They had a great escape; for, in
spite of the nicety of the nurseryman's packing, five of the pots were smashed
to atoms in that vile railway. Luckily the plants were not injured; they were
planted forthwith, and doubtless will blow, if not next summer, the summer
after. Oh, how I wish you were near enough to come often and see their
growth! and that I in return could see your nosegays, human and floral. Mrs
Bell was charmed with your boys. But they can't help being pretty. The more
you see of her the more you will like her; she is so able, and has all sorts of
knowledge. She was charmed with you.

To Mrs Hoare, Monkstown, Ireland

Swallowfield, Autumn 1852

Thank you, my dearest Mrs Hoare, for the touching French verses, and the touching English prose story. All dogs follow me too! It is strange. I have one here, a young retriever called Seal, really belonging to a son of my kind neighbour, Sir Henry Russell, but who has adopted me. I suppose when he comes to be old enough to go a-shooting that he will discover that I am no sportswoman, but at present he sticks to my skirts (he's just like a shaggy young bear) and won't go away. I like him, and he knows it. Fanchon holds him in high scorn, and he returns the compliment. Thanks for the bog-myrtle; it is still fragrant; but of all fragrance that of the night-scented orchis you mention is most exquisite. The wild hyacinth, dear Mrs Hoare, differs much from the flower which we call the harebell in England: a small campanula, bearing two or three exquisite, thin, bell-like papery flowers (you can hear them rustle when shaken) on a very thin and fragile stalk, growing among wild thyme, and under heather, in the month of August. There is a white variety cultivated in gardens, but no pink one. I have heard both the harebell and the wild hyacinth called blue-bells. As to botany, my knowledge is very scanty; I, like you, love flowers for their beauty and their odour.

To Mrs Acton Tindal, Aylesbury

Swallowfield, 2 August 1852

Ah! my dearest friend! I see that you do not know how very ill I have been. Just before the hot weather set in I was seized with fever, which kept me confined to my bed above a month; and, although I now get up every day, and take a slow drive through our quiet lanes, my recovery is very lingering, and, till the last two days, when I am really mending, I have been one day mending and another day worse. However, although I have had a great shake, and Mr Harness, who came down to see me last week, thinks me breaking fast (as, indeed, everybody's manner says, although their words may not), yet I myself think there is some life in me yet . . . .

Dear Mrs Robert Dering! Never in my life have I had a greater shock than in hearing of her death, whilst myself confined to my bed; we had not met, but we had corresponded almost weekly, and there was about her letters a sweet affectionateness, a grace of heart and mind, such as I have rarely seen equalled. It was a charm quite personal – a charm like a breath of flowers. She had been suffering from neuralgia, and her last letter to me was written in pencil. Then came her death. Hearing of your kindness about the climbing roses, she would send me some herself, so she went to another famous garden and desired the two best unnamed seedlings of last year, and two others, to be sent to me, the two former to be called the Miss Mitford and the Swallowfield; and there they are, dearest friend, mingled with your equally precious trees (none of either package has failed in spite of the unfavourable spring), there they are blossoming underneath the window, whilst the kind heart that sent them lies cold. Ah! Take care of yourself, my precious friend!

To Mrs Hoare, Monkstown, Ireland

Swallowfield, Spring 1853

I do, indeed, adopt you, dearest Mrs Hoare, as 'a friend upon paper' – a true and dear friend! My best and most congenial habits of association and intercourse have so begun; and I do not think that I have ever lost one, who has so taken to me and to whom I have so taken. As to differences of opinion – why the first condition of social intercourse seems to me to be, to agree to differ. I am an old woman, and have always had friends of all parties; and really I hardly know which may count the greater number of gifted and excellent persons. For my own part, I am of no extreme – just midway between dear Mrs Browning, who is a furious Radical, and dear Mrs Jennings, who is an equally furious Tory. We have twenty subjects of dispute, at the very least, to which, if conversation flags, we can resort ding-dong. But I have a notion that party disputes in Ireland are much more inveterate than in England; as, indeed, they have lasted for centuries, and have all the elements of different religions, as well as different races, to promote the discord.

Thank you for the capital sketch (your own – it is an amplification of the Castle Rackrent scenes, which Lever also paints so well) and for Callanan's poems. What a beautiful wild country that Lodge of yours is in! Ah! I know how flowers get local names. I was told the other day that the delicate campanula, which we call the *hare*bell, ought to be *hair*bell, from the little fibrous membrane which does give a hairy aspect to its dry, graceful, pendulous flowers. For my part I accept the common names of flowers, and abjure, above all things, the pedantry of being over-right. I thought you might have a *pink* variety in a soil and climate different from ours and more favourable to vegetation. Our harebell belongs to turfy, sandy commons – the lovely commons which, I am sorry to say, are fast disappearing in our country.

Did I tell you that I am just now almost crippled with rheumatism in knees and ankles, which not only lames me completely, but keeps me prisoner. I

live quite alone, having no relations – almost literally none, except a few distant relations too grand to claim. Many kind friends I have – some of them persons of note in literature; but I think I prefer those who love letters without actually following the trade of authorship – the intelligent audience to the actors on the stage. Adieu, dear friend!

To Mrs Acton Tindal, London

Swallowfield, 9 June 1853

. . . I can never thank you half enough, dearest friend, for your unwearied kindness and attention – a kindness all the greater, that this wet winter and ungenial Spring have made both plants and chickens rarities hereabout. Thank you, dear friend, again and again. I trust that your own Manor House is increasing in the beauty that you love to give, and ought to enjoy. This has been a year of years for flowering trees, lilacs, rhododendrons, azaleas, wisterias, horse-chestnuts. Have you the scarlet horse-chestnut? and does it grow kindly and blossom freely. When it does so, I really think that it is the most gorgeous of English trees, clothed in those rich red pyramidal flowers, but it has bad tricks – it dies, it dwarfs off, it refuses to blossom. And have you the pink lily of the valley? – less pretty than the white, but still charming – and the straw-colour, have you that? I heard of it the other day, at Lord Charlemont's place, in Ireland. Lady Russell, who brought the pink variety from Paris just after the Coronation of Charles X, and after its blowing for a year or two lost it. She says that she had a blue one. No doubt the French florist called it blue, but I suspect, on cross-examination that, like so many *soi disant* blue flowers, it was lilac. I only see the flowers that come to me, for although with great difficulty and great pain, I am lifted somehow downstairs and into my little pony carriage, I am so enfeebled, that to go otherwise than a foot's pace through our lanes, causes me pain all over the body for days after, just as if I had been beaten, and pleasant company – the pleasanter the worse – has just the same effect as a quick drive, and leaves me full of pain and weariness. Nevertheless, Mr May says that air will act as a tonic on the long run, and that there is a chance of my getting stronger, so I am looking out for an old-fashioned Bath chair, in which I may be drawn, under a tree, and left there to read or write without fatigue. . . .

To Charles Boner

Swallowfield, June 1853

I began this as soon as I received yours, but was interrupted, and it is now the 26th of June. When the weather lets me (for we have a wet, cold, showery summer), I sit at the corner of my little dwelling, under a superb acacia-tree, laden just now with as many showy tassels as leaves. What a graceful tree the acacia is! waving its delicate foliage, and bending to every breeze like drooping feathers; just underneath it is a dark syringa, with its ivory blossoms – the English orange flower in look and odour. You know, I believe, my love of sweet scents (I can even accept perfumes when I cannot get flowers), and can imagine how much I delight in this mingled fragrance of the syringa and the acacia. Almost all the very fragrant flowers are white – the violet, the narcissus, the cyclamen, the orange, the thousand fruit blossoms, the jessamine, the hyacinth, the Provence rose, the pink, the tuberose, the gardenia, the magnolia – oh, I could never be able to count them all. My love of fragrant flowers brought me last night a singular visitor.

When putting me to bed K. broke into a variety of exclamations, pointing all the while to the candlestick. Looking as she directed, I saw there a dark-looking caterpillar. It moved, and there was the reflection of a tiny green light. It was a glow-worm. On the table were jars of pinks and roses, and there had been a jar of wild honeysuckle. Doubtless the insect had dropped from the flowers. After some consultation we extinguished the candle, and Sam deposited the candlestick on the turf in front of the house. Ten minutes after, the glow-worm had crawled to the grass, I hope to live out its little life in peace and comfort. Was it not strange? K., who knows my old love for those stars of the earth, says that now I cannot go to them they come to me.

To Miss Jephson, Castle Martyr, Ireland

Swallowfield, July 1854

. . . Yes, dearest Emily, I have most beautiful roses. I found some of the old
sorts and brought some of that exquisite rose *des quatre saisons* which smells
so exactly like the attar of roses, moss roses, maiden blush, double Scotch,
and many others. Then my only expense was for thirty of the very best
standards, some low, some high. Then my house was planted by two
Hertfordshire friends, and the trees are now climbing above the parlour

windows, and will soon cover the house with the very choicest sorts. Then I have a rose hedge round the front court, so you see we abound. There is a moss maiden blush which in beauty, in fragrance, and in mossiness excels anything I ever saw. I don't know its name, but it is more beautiful than either the pink or the white moss rose, fond as I am of the first. I have also a white globe which is more beautiful than any I ever saw, purer, rounder, more perfect in every way, it was sent to me years ago by poor Mr Milton, Mrs Trollope's brother. All the gardeners say it is the best white they ever saw. I have told Sam to send you a plant of this rose, and roots of the *Fleur de lys*, and the double wood anemone. Have you these pretty flowers? I only wish I knew how to make over to you my other roses, but I fear they would not travel. You must write to tell Sam how to send flower roots when the time comes, and he can add those common and fragrant white pinks which will grow like a weed. Rare flowers I have none, and my little pit has only served to keep alive scarlet geraniums, and common verbenas, fuchsias, &c., for planting out. Still my little garden, full of fruit and flowers (the vegetables being kept out of sight), quite cottage-like, pleases everybody, and Miss Mary runs about in it all the day long. After passing eighteen months with the reputation of being the best and quietest child possible, she has taken to crying after her father, who spoils her more than the rest, and whom she cannot bear out of her sight. I do hope that your sweet Emmy and she will some day know each other. The other day I had an interesting account of the Alhambra from a friend just returned from Spain. The exquisite fretted work of the ceilings &c. has faded quite white except in a very few shaded places. Enough, however, of the colours remains there to enable the patterns to be made out, and Government are going to restore these magnificent works to as nearly their old state as possible. Nothing ever approached their lightness, delicacy, and beauty. The imitation in the Crystal Palace is like, they say, but conveys no idea of their matchless grace. I am a little revived by the sweet summer air which breathes around me through the open window.

To John Ruskin

25 November 1854

. . . I have just been reading the report of your lecture in the 'Globe', most kindly sent to me for that purpose by Lady Russell, and I have been so much struck with a coincidence between your knowledge and my ignorance that I cannot help writing to you on the subject. One of my delights in my poor father's life-time, when that acre of garden behind our little cottage was as closely set with flowers as a meadow is set with grass, was to arrange those flowers in jars, and I always found that the way to make a brilliant spot, a bit of colour that did your heart good, was to make the foundation white. Half-open roses amongst white pinks are delicious both to the scent and the sight. The Duke of Devonshire (almost the only great man whom I know, and who has always been so kind to me that I do not apologise for seeming to boast of his kindness, as I should of any other Duke), once brought me a nosegay composed in the same spirit – about a dozen forced moss-rose buds in the centre surrounded by some hundred flower-stalks of the lovely lily of the valley, no leaves, and indeed I generally found that leaves of any sort, even the stemmage and stalkage of the lily, dimmed the colour. This bouquet was really ducal in fragrance and beauty, but my common pinks looked as well, perhaps better, with moss-roses or the dear old cottage rose, had a fine spicy odour and the great merit of coming at the same time and lasting for weeks, sometimes for months. Ask your own dear mother to try this next summer. I dare say that little common pink which grows like a weed is not choice enough for her garden, so you must come and fetch some roots from mine. By far the most gorgeous flower-jar that I ever made was of double white narcissus studded with choice ranunculuses, not hanging loose but packed tightly together. White hollyhocks too mixed with others of rich colour either in a tall jar with all their long spikes, for the bud of the hollyhock is beautiful and so is the peculiar green looking like a daisied lawn on a dewy morning – either in that form or the single blossoms laid closely together in a china dish are very bright and gay. So are dahlias, and dahilas look especially well arranged in a china bowl with a wire frame of the same sphere-like form, into which to insert the stalks. It makes a splendid globe of colour. In the autumn the magnolia grandiflora raising its sculpturesque beauty with a border of fuchsias and other gay flowers drooping round it is very graceful, and for a wild nosegay you will find the white water-lily surrounded by the purple willow-herb, the yellow loose-strife, the deep rose-colour of the ragged robin and the exquisite blue of the forget-me-not very imposing. I have seen people wondering that such an effect should be produced by wild flowers. But whether for scent or elegance, nothing can surpass a quantity of the meadow-sweet denuded of its leaves and left to the charm of its feathery lightness and its pearly, creamy tint. Forgive this blotted scrawl, dear friend. It is your fault, or rather that of your lecture, and you may imagine how much I was pleased to find myself right without knowing it. One other thing I must mention: leaves injure the scent of many flowers, syringa denuded of them is really almost the orange blossom; the honeysuckle and mignonette also suffer by their vicinity.

To a Friend of Mrs Hoare's

Swallowfield, 7 January 1855

. . . It has pleased Providence to preserve to me my calmness of mind, clearness of intellect, and also my power of reading by day and by night; and, which is still more, my love of poetry and literature, my cheerfulness, and my enjoyment of little things. This very day, not only my common pensioners, the dear robins, but a saucy troop of sparrows, and a little shining bird of passage, whose name I forget, have all been pecking at once at their tray of bread-crumbs outside the window. Poor pretty things! how much delight there is in those common objects, if people would but learn to enjoy them.

The Forget-Me-Not

Blossom that lov'st on shadowy banks to lie,
  Gemming the deep rank grass with flowers so blue,
  That the pure turquoise matched with their rich hue
Pales, fades, and dims; so exquisite a dye,
That scarce the brightness of the Autumn sky,
  Which sleeps upon the bosom of the stream,
  On whose fringed margent thy star-flowerets gleam
In its clear azure with thy tints may vie;
  Shade-loving flower, I love thee! not alone
That thou dost haunt the greenest coolest spot,
  For ever, by the tufted alder thrown,
Or arching hazel, or vine mantled cot,
  But that thy very name hath a sweet tone
Of parting tenderness – Forget me not!

from *Dramatic Scenes, Sonnets, and Other Poems,* 1827

LIST OF ILLUSTRATIONS